Aesop's Anthropol

Aesop's Anthropology

A Multispecies Approach

John Hartigan Jr.

University of Minnesota Press

Minneapolis

Introduction

Welcome to *Aesop's Anthropology: A Multispecies Approach*,[1] an effort to theorize culture and society across species lines. This project pursues a basic question: what can we learn about culture from other species? Studies of nonhumans are generating new perspectives on intelligence, media, and networking, but they've yet to impact how we understand sociality.[2] This is largely because of the notion that culture uniquely characterizes us as a species—much like racial and classed conceits equated *culture* and *cultivation* with the highest achievements of European society in the last millennium. But this is also attributable to the dependence of social theorists on the notion of social construction. In this view, we only ever engage nonhumans through representations, reflections of our cultural conditioning and social order. But the usefulness of social construction—along with certainty about the uniqueness of humans—has eroded.[3] It's time to recognize that sociality, in its origins and elaborations, begins with nonhumans. We're late to the game of culture, and it's time to catch up in our thinking about the social.

This is an apt moment for such an undertaking because social theory seems either to be dissolving or rapidly fragmenting. Out of this moment, a range of "new directions" or "turns" is growing quickly: the ontological turn, posthumanism, speculative materialism, affect or non-representational theory,[4] and of course, the species turn.[5] These turns commonly shift away from social *explanans* and objects: classes, races, and nations; economics, politics, and institutions.[6] Each also variously rejects a focus on culture defined as comprising webs of meaning from which representations of the world are generated and transmitted—by humans. *Aesop's Anthropology* makes a different case: that we still need culture; the concept retains many analytical uses. Some of these are crucial to the central problematic of the twenty-first century: negotiating the line between human and nonhuman. The key step in renewing the uses of culture is *to reverse the trajectory by which social theory is generated*—through meticulous speculation about and observations of humans—and start anew, shedding the assumption that society and culture begin with, or are principally about, people.

Social theorists have settled on too narrow a view of sociality by considering the unique case of humans. The central premise here is that *cultural* anthropology should principally be concerned with understanding culture, not just the "Man" or *Anthro,* which has stood at the center of efforts to define this concept. We've drawn a too limited domain of the social by focusing on humans principally, then regarding nonhuman forms as rudimentary or primitive.[7] We have to flip this to think the social without privileging the exceptional case of humans, to arrive at an understanding of cultural dynamics that currently is not part of our thinking about sociality. After all, humans may not be the optimum locus for understanding the social because (1) we're only one among many social species and (2) we've got a skewed (anthropocentric) version of culture. But how to do this without totemizing "natural" objects to reify social categories, as with the poignant case of race and the dehumanization of people as simians, insects, and a variety of disparaged domesticated species?

Aesop's Anthropology addresses these questions and others via a series of forays into analytical topics, linked efforts to rethinking sociality by following examples of culture across species lines. The forays are arrayed as follows: "Are Natives Plants or People?" ponders the uses and perils of terms that refer just as easily to humans and nonhumans; "Nonhuman Cultures," as the title suggests, reviews the range of research that ruptures the "golden barrier" reserving culture for humans;[8] "The Social (re)Turn" samples foundational moments of theorizing the social when the line constituting this barrier was either breached or drawn; and "Diversity" considers problems that arise when not maintaining this line, particularly with race, as discourses for managing species become a means for "domesticating" racial conflict.

The problem and dynamics here run deeper than race as an historical artifact—one that likely arises with animal domestication rather than with an "idea of race" attributed to Enlightenment thinkers. Through this view of deep time, "Horticultural Hermeneutic" considers how human thought has yet to escape its fundamental dependence on nonhuman life-forms, such as plants; "Webs without Meaning" considers what this

mode of thought might produce—besides meaningful social constructions—as it moves beyond regarding select life-forms totemically. "What
Is a Garden?" takes up matters of metaphors, parallels, and intuitions
of sameness that arise in pondering nonhuman cultural forms; and
"Homology" addresses the rigorous epistemological means for honing
such intuitions into factual claims and hypotheses.

"Species Thinking" recounts the historical developments that allow us
to shift from regarding nonhumans as just "good to think" with[9] to considering other life-forms as means of defining the cultural—that which
takes up a variety of materials "to think with" in the first place. This is
difficult to do, and "The Fables as Form" highlights the allegorical tendencies that inform accounts of multispecies encounters; these tendencies are fully evident in the important role that "Model Organisms" play
in the production of scientific knowledge. More broadly, "Species in the
News" considers the selective (i.e., cultural) ways some species get coverage while others do not. What potential exists for such stories to be more
than about us humans? The answer turns, increasingly, on technologies
for "Identifying Species," in particular, DNA bar coding, which is dis-
placing epistemological practices and projects with a simple technique of
recognition. The commercial dimensions of this technology rest on the
foundational ground of "Domestication," that domain in which human
and nonhuman are deeply entangled, coproducing one another. But this
is not just a domain where species meet; this is where the plasticity and
dynamism of species become fodder for cultivation, in a still-uncertain
confusion of multidirectional causal arrows and muddled agencies. "Have
Culture, Will Travel" takes up E. O. Wilson's arguments in *The Social Conquest of the Earth* to frame cultivation, rather than culture more generally,
as the really challenging dynamic to think about across species lines.[10]
"Furthermore," wraps up this initial stage of theorizing culture from a
multispecies perspective by highlighting core features of this concept
that become apparent in considering transspecies forms of sociality.

Each of these forays will be further elaborated and explored in serial
fashion in time to come at aesopsanthropology.com. This approach to
theorizing is purposefully open. Subjects like "animal culture," for
instance, are contentious and unsettled, involving ongoing research
claims and counterclaims but also a steady "unthinking" of certain
assumptions. New studies have the potential to generate different directions in theorizing, or perhaps to shift previous epistemological configurations. Also, the core questions raised here are better not answered
emphatically. What units of analysis reliably allow us to think across and

between species? What kind of explanatory register does *culture* or *social* provide? What do we refer to and assume when we mobilize these terms?

What better figure for pondering all this than Aesop,[11] He also records that Aesop was a slave who perhaps gained his freedom through a remarkable eloquence and ability to spin tales. Possibly, too, he died at Delphi, where he was sent on a diplomatic mission by King Croesus of Lydia and where, after insulting the Delphians, he was thrown from a cliff. Certainly, though, he had a long career or afterlife as a trickster figure in Europe, beginning in the thirteenth century with *Life of Aesop*, composed by Maximus Planudes in Constantinople. This version of the storyteller features episodes of his life—usually involving a wicked wit that repeatedly lands him in trouble—that once were as well savored as the fables attributed to him. But maybe he is only a name with the power to attract stories that form an enduring genre, one avidly transmitted across three millennia.

A central feature of these stories is the capacity for nonhumans—living beings or objects—to act and speak in ways that reveal some larger truth, perhaps about humans or maybe more properly about life itself. They figure a particular capability to inspire intuitions and perceptions of commonalities with nonhumans. Aesop, "by announcing a story which everyone knows not to be true, told the truth by the very fact that he did not claim to be relating real events."[12] Aesop is an apt figure—because he offered up nonhumans as objects of thought—to serve as guide in orienting cultural anthropology to think anew about nonhumans, where it's not so much a question of getting *beyond the human* as it is pondering what lies *between us and them.*

Notes

1.   http://www.aesopsanthropology.com/blog/.

2.   Justin Greg, "A New Frontier in Animal Intelligence," *Scientific American,* October 13, 2013; Jussi Parikka, *Insect Media: An Archaeology of Animals and Technology,* Posthumanities 11 (Minneapolis: University of Minnesota Press, 2010); Thierry Bardini, *Junkware,* Posthumanities 13 (Minneapolis: University of Minnesota Press, 2011).

3.   Ian Hacking, *The Social Construction of What?* (Cambridge, Mass.: Harvard University Press, 2000); John Hartigan, "Is Race Still Socially Constructed? The Recent Controversy over Race and Medical Genetics," *Science as Culture* 17, no. 2 (2008): 163.

4. See Morten Axel Pedersen and Martin Holbraad, "The Politics of Ontology," January 13, 2014, http://www.culanth.org/fieldsights/461-the-politics-of-ontology; Cary Wolfe, *What Is Posthumanism?* Posthumanities 8 (Minneapolis: University of Minnesota Press, 2010); Levi Bryant, Nick Srnicek, and Graham Harman, eds., *The Speculative Turn: Continental Materialism and Realism* (Melbourne, Australia: re.press, 2011); Nigel Thrift, *Non-representational Theory: Space, Politics, Affect* (New York: Routledge, 2008).

5. On this rapidly developing mode of inquiry, see Eben Kirksey and Stefan Helmreich, "The Emergence of Multispecies Ethnography," *Cultural Anthropology* 25, no. 4 (2010): 545–76; Jasbir Puar and Julie Livingston, *Interspecies* (Durham, N.C.: Duke University Press, 2011); Laura A. Ogden, Billy Hall, and Kimiko Tanita, "Animals, Plants, People, and Things: A Review of Multispecies Ethnography," *Environment and Society: Advances in Research* 4, no. 1 (2013): 5–24; Rhoda Wilkie, "Multispecies Scholarship and Encounters: Changing Assumptions at the Human–Animal Nexus," *Sociology*, July 2013.

6. See Bruno Latour, *Reassembling the Social: An Introduction to Actor-Network-Theory* (Oxford: Oxford University Press, 2007), and Bruno Latour and Catherine Porter, *Politics of Nature: How to Bring the Sciences into Democracy* (Cambridge, Mass.: Harvard University Press, 2004).

7. The "we" invoked here generally references fellow cultural anthropologists but also sometimes refers to conspecifics.

8. Christophe Boesch, "Is Culture a Golden Barrier between Human and Chimpanzee?" *Evolutionary Anthropology: Issues, News, and Reviews* 12, no. 2 (2003): 82–91.

9. Claude Lévi-Strauss, *Totemism* (Boston: Beacon Press, 1971).

10. Edward O. Wilson, *The Social Conquest of Earth* (New York: Liveright, 2012).

11. http://en.wikipedia.org/wiki/Aesop.[footnote] a Greek storyteller (circa 620 and 560 bce) of whom much is rumored and little is known? No writings by Aesop survive, but Herodotus identified him as "the fable writer."[footnote]Herodotus, *The Histories*, Penguin Classics L34 (Baltimore, Md.: Penguin Books, 1960).

12. Philostratus, *Life of Apollonius of Tyana*, Book V:14.

1

Are Natives Plants or People?

The impetus for this project was a comment by James Clifford in an informal workshop in the Department of Anthropology at the University of Texas at Austin in 2006. Clifford was discussing research on his book *Returns: Becoming Indigenous in the Twenty-First Century*.[1] As an aside, he noted, "Thirty years ago, if you looked up *indigenous* in the dictionary you'd probably find mostly plants. Now it's a whole class of people." The idea that our current racial use of *indigenous* shifted from a means of characterizing plants to a means of identifying people riveted my thinking and soon informed my attention to genomics projects on humans and maize in Mexico.[2] Principally, it began to destabilize my expectation that there is a prior ground of culture by which the elements of nature are taken up and manipulated. As well, it led me to glimpse the potential value of a term like *indigenous,* or *native,* because of its mobility across species lines, exactly for its capacity to refer similarly to both people and plants. But this is a risky subject.

The problem, of course, is that this capacity is fundamentally racialized. Natives, as people, are an enduring concern of anthropology. For much of the discipline's history, natives were anthropologists' central subject matter; we studied exotic, often "primitive" peoples in remote corners of the world. In doing so, the discipline largely hewed to European colonialist projects and objectives, in which natives were administrative subjects, often unruly and inscrutable. Today *indigenous* somewhat updates an interest in natives, claiming a position of otherness as a source of identity and mobilization. The terms both are racialized, but like reclaimed identities such as *queer* or *redneck, indigenous* revoices a pejorative as a political stance. But for a good deal longer, both terms and concepts have borne an immodest, licentious capacity to refer to plants as well as people.

What to make of this ontological promiscuity, especially given the racial dimension of both *native* and *indigenous*? Viewed via the history of colonialism, *native,* principally is the category by which Europeans racially differentiated themselves from the peoples they were colonizing. And this highlights exactly why social theorists are so keen to draw a line between human and nonhuman—because race is assumed to depend on naturalization of social categories. But the racial dynamic here is not quite so straightforward. Europeans, too, were "natives," specifically in a linguistic sense, as "native speakers" of the languages and their publics that were playing a central role in ratifying and embodying nationalism. This version of *natives* was about establishing forms of sameness rather than difference—similarities in how language was acquired in relation to place and birth. The willingness, even eagerness, of Europeans to identify as natives is matched by many of my fellow Anglo Texans who sport bumper stickers asserting their status as "native Texan," over and against people like me, who arrived more recently.

Native, from its Latin root, designates a condition of belonging at and by birth to both a place and a group—a nation, say, by *nātiō*—from which we also derive *nature* or *nātūra*: "birth, constitution, character, and generative potential" *(Oxford English Dictionary)*. There are connections to the soil implied or assumed here, which brings up the contrasting concept of cultivation—an act that transforms a state of nature. Interestingly, though, cultivation has this same capacity to apply to people and plants: the agricultural act became the model for the transformative power of education and training, or culture, that which we transmit socially rather than inherit genetically. We derive the very idea of talking about people as cultural from immemorial labor of ancient humans with plants. If we were to assume that the doubling capacity of *native* is problematic because it involves the belief that both plants and people have initial, natural states, then what to make of the similar equivocality of its presumed opposite terms, *cultivation* or *culture*?

The tendency among social theorists when confronting the racial aspect of native is, first, to assume a one-way traffic of signification and, second, to call it to a halt. Hugh Raffles protested the use of *native* and *invasive* with regard to plants because the terms fuel anti-immigrant sentiment in the United States.[3] John and Jean Comaroff made a similar argument concerning South Africa, where they heard, in discussions of threatened native species of plants, "an instance of 'ideology in the making'"—where "the anxiety over foreign flora gestured toward a submerged landscape of civic terror and moral alarm."[4] In each instance, social analysis leads to the conclusion that discussions about plants are really—ideologically—about people; the equivocal referents of *native* simply allow a racial ideology to flow effectively from nature to culture. An end result of this analysis, though, is that we end up only ever talking about humans, and it's devilishly hard to consider the plants without viewing them as discursive representation.

But consider that the multireferential capacity of *native* is not a means of ratifying forms of racial difference; instead—or at least additionally—it is an intuition about fundamental commonalities between human and nonhuman, or perhaps of the fundamental instability of delineating nature and culture. This is what Stefan Helmreich relates in *Alien Ocean: Anthropological Voyages in Microbial Seas*, a multifaceted ethnographic account of oceanography.[5] In posing the matter of "How Scientists Think: About 'Natives,' for Example," Helmreich relates, "The scientists of whom I have written so far think about natives in ways that call upon nature and culture even as they demonstrate the instability of this distinction."[6] Plants and people can all be natives—just as we can both be cultivated—because we share forms of sameness that transgress a philosophical and political delineation of the human from everything else. To get at that commonality and how it is imagined and interpreted, we need more than a social analysis that assumes all of this is just racial discourse.[7] This capacity lies await exactly in terms, such as *native*, that can go both ways. Rather than principally serving to ratify (via naturalizing) social categories and hierarchies, *native* and *indigenous* open breaches in an understanding of the social as that which keeps us distinct from every other living thing. *Aesop's Anthropology* begins from this opening, eschewing the ideological approach of clarifying the perceptual order of *native* in relation to race and humans and instead attending avidly to its promiscuous capacity to refer simultaneously and in an undifferentiated manner to plants and people.

In social analysis, with culture (human) on one side and nature (nonhuman) on the other, terms like *native* and *indigenous* will always be suspect, and the critical "intervention" will be to sunder or "clarify" their fluid passage across this line. But this delineation does not match the careers of either term, the emergence of which well predates the idea that humans even have culture (see "Have Culture, Will Travel"). Their usage, historically and currently, and their capacity to refer simultaneously to people and plants disrupts the tendency to theorize the social strictly in terms of humans. The value of *native* and *indigenous* lies in reminding that culture and nature are intertwined such that we can use them to identify transspecies dynamics and homologous structures. At a moment when questions of the nonhuman matter greatly, we have to avail ourselves of the *opportunity of finding in our critical and analytical discourses a leveling effect* similar to that achieved by Darwin's theory of evolution—to remove the conceptual boundaries that wall humans off from all other life-forms on the planet.

The capacity of these terms is even greater considering the shift in scale they permit, by bringing into view the microbiotic realms as well. Microbes, too, can be indigenous—of a place—as well as cosmopolitan, world travelers. Increasingly, farmers and environmentalists concoct means of cultivating "stews"[8] of indigenous microbes that hasten composting or improve the health of plant life.[9] Conversely, biogeographers recognize the enormous range of mobility that microorganisms possess, as they follow distribution patterns that may alternately dwarf or parallel the migrations of humans and animals and the colonizing activities of plants and ants. In "The Anthropology of Microbes," Benezra and colleagues envision approaching "indigenous microbial populations" by "incorporating anthropological analyses into the design and interpretation of studies of human microbial ecology."[10] The traffic here is decidedly two-way: microbes shift "fundamental questions of relatedness, selfhood, and social transformation that have long been, and still remain, central to anthropological study," while "investigating microbes from an ethnographic perspective should provide anthropologists with new perspectives about how human biology and social practices are inextricable."[11] In this view, cultural analysis is not directed toward how humans think about nonhumans but rather shifts from a previous insistence on culture being distinct from biology to now thinking in expressly biocultural terms.[12]

Notes

1. James Clifford, *Returns: Becoming Indigenous in the Twenty-First Century* (Cambridge, Mass.: Harvard University Press, 2013).

2. John Hartigan, "Mexican Genomics and the Roots of Racial Thinking," *Cultural Anthropology* 28, no. 2 (2013): 372–95.

3. "Mother Nature's Melting Pot," *New York Times*, April 3, 2011, www.nytimes.com/2011/04/03/opinion/03Raffles.html.

4. Jean Comaroff and John Comaroff, "Naturing the Nation: Aliens, Apocalypse and the Postcolonial State," *Journal of Southern African Studies* 27, no. 3 (2001): 629, 630. Also see a more recent op-ed by Raffles, "Speaking Up for the Mute Swans in Long Island Sound," *New York Times*, February 17, 2014.

5. Stefan Helmreich, *Alien Ocean: Anthropological Voyages in Microbial Seas* (Berkeley: University of California Press, 2010).

6. Ibid., 159.

7. Helmreich confronts this in asking "how do biologists define native?" observing that, "far from being a straightforward matter of biological classification, this is a taxing taxonomic question, especially in Hawai'i, where the word for native resonates with descriptors used by and for the indigenous people of Hawai'i, known as Native Hawaiians." Analytically, he resolves this by framing these as parataxis (parallel classifications) and offering "parataxonomic thinking as a conceptual instrument to show how nature/culture, native/alien, science/politics always shape on another." Ibid., 149, 169.

8. http://rverzola.wordpress.com/agriculture-2/indigenous-microorganisms-imo/.

9. Hoon Park and Michael DuPonte, "How to Cultivate Indigenous Microorganisms," *Biotechnology,* August 2008, BIO-9 published by the College of Tropical Agriculture and Human Resources (CTAHR), University of Hawai'i at Mānoa, Honolulu.

10. Amber Benezra, Joseph DeStefano, and Jeffrey I. Gordon, "Anthropology of Microbes," *Proceedings of the National Academy of Sciences of the United States of America* 109, no. 17 (2012): 6378.

11. Ibid.

12. See Tim Ingold and Gisli Palsson, *Biosocial Becomings: Integrating Social and Biological Anthropology* (New York: Cambridge University Press, 2013). Also see John Hartigan, "Introduction" and "Conclusion," in *Anthropology of Race: Genes, Biology, and Culture* (Santa Fe, N.M.: School of Advanced Research, 2013).

2

Nonhuman Cultures

Did you know, they have it too, culture? Not everyone does—that is, not all species are social, *and* the notion of nonhuman culture is not widely shared. But the evidence of cultures "beyond the human" is copious and growing, though it remains contentious.[1] The question of whether or how culture operates homologously (see "Homology") across species lines highlights some of the keenest anxieties about the status of the human in relation to social theory. For all the uncertainty and vagueness around the culture concept in relation to people, it remains a touchstone for insisting on forms of absolute difference with the nonhuman. Though the concept of culture has been oft disparaged by cultural anthropologists, that disregard quickly dissipates when it comes to the question of whether animals have culture too.[2] Suddenly, culture matters very much and is easily legible, even privileged, in characterizing us as a species. Partly this is due to the dominance of models based on language for analyzing culture. If animals don't have it—a disputed point—then they can't possibly have culture. Also, we're loath to give up being meaning bound as a hallmark of our species (see "Webs without Meaning"). So a sort of arrogance and anthropocentrism construes the very question as dubious and deluded. At the same time, this remains a highly anxiety-producing domain for critical forms of social theory, because this is where parallels between humans and nonhumans gain traction in naturalizing or rationalizing particular social configurations and dynamics (see "Diversity").

But the possibilities and options for thinking and deploying culture across species lines are just too many and too generative to foreclose by maintaining the uniqueness of humanity through retention of culture as a singular possession. What do recognitions of nonhuman cultures allow us to think? Many things, in tandem. First, they present a means of regarding nonhumans as part of a continuum we share with them, of greater and lesser degrees of enculturation. Second, this is an opportunity to think comparatively about the capacity of culture both to respond to and to alter ecologies and biologies. In breaching the "golden barrier" that construes culture as a unique possession of humans, we can begin to think more broadly about the power and pervasiveness of culture—that force or condition that has altered the globe, as in the emergence of the Anthropocene (see "Domestication"). Together, these reasons generatively combine to give social theorists a means and cause to reconsider culture as something more than that befuddling medium through which ideology operates. But let's initially take these in turn.

In the decades since the idea of nonhuman cultures was broached, the notion has taken hold through recognitions that *they* also can learn and transmit social knowledge. As Andrew Whiten, Kevin Laland, and their colleagues explain, the presence of "social learning" and "traditions and other culturally related phenomena" among nonhumans has "proved to be far more widespread across the animal kingdom than imagined a half-century ago and more complex in their manifestations."[3] That's partly because the list of such creatures is sprawling: numerous vertebrates—horses and hyenas, bats and crows, dolphins and dogs, all kinds of cats and rodents, and of course, our closest cousins, the primates—and the most globally dominant invertebrate genera: ants and termites, bees and wasps, and even some spiders. But this also reflects shifting sensibilities among researchers that what we observe other species doing is not a matter of anthropocentric projection but rather a fairly accurate perception of homologous activities.

Thinking this way requires a simple, mobile analytic that applies widely across species and foundationally to humans as well. Gabriel de Tarde's work, which has seen a recent surge of new interest, is useful because he equates the social with two basic capacities: *innovation* and *imitation.* These are also the two prominent units of analysis for considering nonhuman forms of culture today.[4] Mimesis, that long-running concern in cultural analysis, is directly applicable as a transspecies dynamic; the question is largely, what are the mediums through which imitation both operates and is socially transmitted? The answer is ready at hand: researchers working with nonhumans tend to focus on vocalizations (as communicative systems) and foraging (behavioral interactions with a larger environment).

These two topics matter because there is increasing evidence that these are learned and passed on within certain species. Many cetaceans (like dolphins and whales) as well as birds develop "local" dialects—patterned forms of vocalization that help groups cohere and reproduce, and that are neither inherited nor transmitted biologically. These calls or sounds are acquired by conspecifics and play a role in where and how groups forage. Their vocalizations convey patterns of information acquired from and applied to environmental settings. Presumably, such communication also involves an interpretive dimension, in interpreting both environmental contexts and conspecific interactions with that same context. But as this brings us close to meaning, does this perspective, in focusing so keenly on modes of communication, rely on or risk inscribing an anthropocentric definition of culture?

The answer will depend on how all of this works vis-à-vis biology, that long-running foil for articulating the social and our well-ensconced domain for identifying the real. What matters here is the realization that culture, which we've largely equated with the generation of symbolic thought and the operation of meaning, in a mentalist-bound sensibility, may be *far more deeply entangled with biology* than the "mind" imagined. Think of the various turns today—ontological, affect, nonrepresentational: *none of them* opens up the biological in the way that culture potentially can when viewed in this transspecific frame. But the capacity for doing so is where cultural anthropologists may get squeamish. Underlying all this research on the culture of nonhumans is an evolutionary notion of culture, one that "recognizes and exploits parallels between biological and cultural change," a "rigorous science of culture" that draws on evolutionary biology yet is directed at "the specific and unique processes of culture."[5] But wait, isn't "culture" that which separated humans from determinate forms of biology and freed us from strictures of natural selection? Maybe not. But if not, the gain from this line of thought is a much more plastic—that is, less deterministic—version of either biology or evolution.

Making all this more lively, Maurizio Meloni reports that an emergent "'social turn' in the life-sciences is taking shape."[6] "Biology is becoming more social" in its analytical orientation, Meloni observes, pointing to the emergence of a "prosocial view of evolution" (emphasizing roles of cooperation and altruism), a focus in neuroscience on "the social brain" ("a multiply connected device profoundly shaped by social influences") and a postgenomics emphasis on the "socialized gene," as glimpsed in the new field of molecular epigenetics. In each of these development, Meloni claims, "the traditional separation between the biological and the social has become increasingly difficult to define: biology has become porous to social and even cultural signals to an unprecedented extent."[7] And these developments—concerned with a parity between "many interacting inheritance systems" (genetic and biological as well as environmental and cultural)—are not even principally engaging with the slate of research topics derived from social or eusocial species.

Another approach to the question of nonhuman culture begins not with considering how they might do what we do too but rather with the recognition that our version of culture was largely developed entirely through engagements with or attention to nonhumans. Paleoanthropologist Pat Shipman makes the case that "the animal connection"—underlying tool making, symbolic thought and behavior, and domestication of plants and animals—is the basis for humanity.[8] At each of the key moments when our distinctive constitution emerged, nonhumans were there, as impetus or companion species. Tool use developed, Shipman speculates, in conjunction with the carving up of animal carcasses; symbols arose in prehistory to represent the presence and interest in animals, as reflected in numerous cave paintings; and domestication, of course, was predicated on transformations of nonhumans. What would we be now without them? And this is before even raising the point that our dependence on the nonhuman extends to the microbial level. In this approach, culture is not something we find similarly operating in far distant species (evolutionarily speaking) but *something we only achieved through entanglements with proximate ones.*

The gain for cultural analysis is similar in both cases. First, we begin to get at something that has bedeviled social theorists for decades: how do you succinctly define culture? Culture generates adaptive behaviors that have the power to transform environments ("niche construction" or place making) but that also can funnel the flow of genes in a species through mating rituals and kinship dynamics. In this formulation, we also gain a view of culture that is not formed principally by an anthropocentric attachment to meaning. In this view, Kevin Laland explains, "animal culture is much more than a window onto humanity: *it is an evolutionary player.*"[9] "Cultural processes in a broad range of animal species exhibit a number of properties that change the evolutionary dynamic, including detaching the behavior of animals from their ecological environments, generating geographical patterns in phenotypic characters, allowing arbitrary and even maladaptive characters to spreading, influencing evolutionary rates and trajectories, and modifying selection to precipitate and direct evolutionary events."[10] Not only is this an important insight, it is also an impetus to take culture more seriously among humans as well. We need to know more about this powerful dynamic or capacity, and we are best served if we open up the inquiry beyond the human—rather than being reduced to offering copious diagnoses of "neoliberalism," where culture is merely a conduit for the deterministic real of economics and politics (e.g., neoliberal capitalism).

Notes

1. With this phrase, I specifically reference Eduardo Kohn, *How Forests Think: Toward an Anthropology beyond the Human* (Berkeley: University of California Press, 2013), but more broadly, too, a range of efforts at rendering nonhumans as anthropological subjects. See Neil Whitehead, "Post-human Anthropology," *Identities: Global Studies in Culture and Power* 16 (2009): 1–32, and Neil Whitehead and Michael Wesch, *Human No More: Digital Subjectivities, Unhuman Subjects, and the End of Anthropology* (Boulder: University Press of Colorado, 2012) as well as Joanna Latimer and Mara Miele, "Naturecultures? Science, Affect and the Non-Human," *Theory, Culture, and Society* 30, nos. 7–8 (2013): 5–31.

2. I offer a detailed review of this disparagement in "Culture against Race: Reworking the Basis for Racial Analysis," *South Atlantic Quarterly* 104, no. 3 (2005): 543–60.

3. Andrew Whiten, Robert A. Hinde, Kevin N. Laland, and Christopher B. Stringer, "Culture Evolves," *Philosophical Transactions of the Royal Society, Series B, Biological Sciences* 366, no. 1567 (2011): 938–48.

4. L. Lehmann, M. W. Feldman, and R. Kaeuffer, "Cumulative Cultural Dynamics and the Coevolution of Cultural Innovation and Transmission: An ESS Model for Panmictic and Structured Populations," *Journal of Evolutionary Biology* 23, no. 11 (2012): 2356–69.

5. Whiten et al., "Culture Evolves," 939.

6. Maurizio Meloni, "How Biology Became Social, and What It Means for Social Theory," *The Sociological Review* 62 (2014): 3.

7. Ibid., 2.

8. Pat Shipman, *The Animal Connection: A New Perspective on What Makes Us Human* (New York: W. W. Norton, 2011).

9. Kevin Laland, "Animal Cultures," *Current Biology* 18, no. 9 (2008): R367; emphasis added.

10. Ibid., R367.

3

The Social (re)Turn

The history of theorizing the social features a variety of moments when its exclusive assignment to humans was neither assured nor assumed. How has the intuition or perception of the social been constituted via glimpses across the species lines? Interestingly, one of the founding moments of analyzing the social took the form of a fable, Bernard Mandeville's *Fable of the Bees*.[1] The allegory unfolded in a series of iterations—first as satire, then as a theory of sociability in commercial societies, and finally as a fuller philosophical reflection on the transformation of humans from animals into moral entities via the civilizing process.[2] But it built on a perception that informed the concept of the division of labor, one that paralleled a beehive with human society. Adam Smith further developed this intuition, but philosophers such as Kant, Hume, and Rousseau also referenced and mobilized this fable. As E. G. Hundert explains in *The Enlightenment's Fable: Bernard Mandeville and the Discovery of Society*, "in The Fable's anatomy of human motives, the social order could for the first time be analytically isolated and comprehensively understood as a complex, but rule-bound, conjunction of the facts of nature."[3] This *naturalization of society* allowed for "lawlike" forms of social explanation, which were the foundations for fusing "social" and "science."

Today, as thoroughgoing naturalists (see Descola in "Webs without Meaning"), we cringe at such rudimentary forms of thought as suggested in the mobilization of fable. Yet they remain evident and influential in the figures and narratives that inform and permeate social research today.[4] But the case of anthropology is somewhat complicated, because it was able to generate—through ethnographic practice and cultural analysis, deployed in attempts to develop reliable accounts of diverse modes of thought and ways of life—a generative observation: that species can be "good to think."[5] The innovation attempted in *Aesop's* is to shift from this view of species—as merely mediums with which to think about our social orders or positions and cultural conditions—to recognize them rather as revealing something about this mysterious, besetting force, culture, that which anthropology both set out to study and deployed in copious field settings. The idea here is that, through studying transspecies commonalities, we might recognize not the obscure truths of alterity but rather *the way sameness is realized and cultivated.* This entails a certain style of thought that maps very closely with ethnography, one that certainly gives in to allegorical tendencies to see where they may lead.

Long ago, James Clifford demonstrated that "ethnographic texts are inescapably allegorical," that is, a narrative that "continuously refers to another pattern of ideas or event."[6] Even realistic, empirical accounts feature "extended metaphors, patterns of association that point to coherent (theoretical, esthetic, moral) additional meanings," such that "allegory prompts us to say of any cultural description not 'this represents, or symbolizes, that' but rather, 'this is a (morally charged) *story* about that.'" This involves "a *double attention* to the descriptive surface and to more abstract, comparative, explanatory levels of meaning"; "what one sees . . . is connected in a continuous double structure with what one understands."[7] This notion of a doubled attention can be expanded via terms, such as *native, indigenous,* and *population,* that have a capacity to operate similarly in transspecies registers. If the allegorical is unavoidable in fashioning cultural accounts, why not find a way to take the allegorical form more seriously in exactly trying to navigate this fraught transborder activity of crossing the human and nonhuman domains? The challenge is to do so while still producing what we expect of social science: reliable accounts of the social world.

Such dabblings—in allegories, nonhumans, and philosophical ruminations—were largely foreclosed in an initiatory professional gesture of social theory. Emile Durkheim, a founder of sociology and a key figure in the development of anthropology, stands out for delineating the social as distinct from everything else. He formulated the "social fact" as something different from a biological, chemical, or psychological fact. Because, he demonstrated, the social is not reducible to or explained by these other domains. This meant the social had to be taken seriously in its own terms and could not be reductively rendered as a function of biology or the individual psyche. The social comprises "collective representations" that impinge on us, as individuals. Marshal Sahlins elaborated on Durkheim's foundation when he challenged the idea of "sociobiology" that E. O. Wilson promoted,[8] again asserting that there are certain irreducible layers of reality. Physics explains particles and motion; chemistry explains bonds and reactions; biology is about physiology. "Biology, while it is an absolutely necessary condition for culture, is equally and absolutely insufficient" to the task of explaining culture, Sahlins argued, because "it is completely unable to specify cultural properties of human behavior or their variation from one human group to another."[9] That currently "biosociality," an odd inversion of sociobiology, has become such a popular subject of theorizing in anthropology suggests that this version of culture is about to be radically reformulated.

Another indication of this is the surge of interest in one of Durkheim's contemporaries and rivals, Gabriel de Tarde. Bruno Latour hails him "as an early ancestor" for his actor-network theory;[10] Nigel Thrift follows Latour in developing from Tarde's writings the assertion that "everything can be regarded as society";[11] Tony Sampson, in *Virality: Contagion Theory in the Age of Networks,* sees Tarde as crucial to understanding emergent forms like neuromarketing and social networking because his version of the social "made no distinctions between individual persons, animals, insects, bacteria, atoms, cells, or larger societies of events like markets, nations, and cities."[12] Who better to turn to as we grapple with the central insight of the "species turn": that 90 percent of the life mass we identify as human comprises nonhuman cells and genes? But the potential relevance of Tarde is better illustrated by the profound prevalence of his two key terms, *imitation* and *innovation,* in current research on "animal cultures" and nonhuman "social species."

Tarde's formulation of the social featured a mobility of this concept across species lines: "Society may be defined as a group of beings who are apt to imitate one another."[13] What matters here is his willingness, at that moment in the emergence of social theory, to extend it beyond the human. From this core definition, he allowed, "we should not only have to recognize the right of animal groups to be called societies, we should have to admit that they were the societies *par excellence,*" and furthermore, that "among animals themselves, the most typical societies would not be formed by the highest, by bees, ants, horses, and beavers, but by the lowest, by siphonophorae, for example, where division of labor is so complete that eating and digesting are carried on separately by different individuals."[14]

We might say, following Tarde, as Latour does, that "everything is social," but *Aesop's* opts for a more delimited version. Not all animals are social, and certainly not all insects—though some of these are "eusocial,"[15] featuring divisions of labor and cooperative rearing practices. *How such distinctions between species are made needs to be the purview of cultural anthropologists* as well as biologists, not only because of our relevant expertise in studying sociality, but for cautions and concerns regarding moments when these types of parallels play into the ideological operations, particularly with race, that so deeply disquiet social theorists.

Notes

1. Bernard Mandeville, *The Fable of the Bees* (1723; repr., Harmondsworth, U.K.: Penguin, 1970).

2. Norbert Elias, *The Civilizing Process* (Cambridge, Mass.: Blackwell, 1994).

3. E. J. Hundert, *The Enlightenment's Fable: Bernard Mandeville and the Discovery of Society* (New York, N.Y.: Cambridge University Press, 1994), 60.

4. John Hartigan, *Odd Tribes: Toward an Analysis of White People* (Durham, N.C.: Duke University Press, 2005).

5. Lévi-Strauss, *Totemism*.

6. James Clifford, *Writing Culture: The Poetics and Politics of Ethnography: A School of American Research Advanced Seminar*, ed. James Clifford and George E. Marcus (Berkeley: University of California Press, 1986), 99–100.

7. Ibid., 101, emphasis added.

8. E. O. Wilson, *Sociobiology: The New Synthesis* (Cambridge, Mass.: Belknap Press of Harvard University Press, 1975).

9. Marshall D. Sahlins, *The Use and Abuse of Biology: An Anthropological Critique of Sociobiology* (Ann Arbor: University of Michigan Press, 1976), xi.

10. Latour, *Reassembling the Social*, 13–15.

11. Thrift, *Non-representational Theory*, 21.

12. Tony D. Sampson, *Virality: Contagion Theory in the Age of Networks* (Minneapolis: University of Minnesota Press, 2012), 6.

13. Gabriel Tarde, *Laws of Imitation* (Charleston, S.C.: BiblioBazaar, 2009), 68.

14. Ibid., 60.

15. See Wilson, *Sociobiology*, chapter 15.

4

Diversity

On a recent frosty morning, I found an e-mail in my inbox announcing the formation of a university-wide "Campus Climate Response Team." I assumed this was some new green initiative or that it had to do with building temperatures (which are always too cold) or broken plumbing fixtures, as we were in a drought and water was growing scarce, partly because of leaky old pipes. These connotations make sense when you are sitting in new building that proudly proclaims its Leadership in Energy and Environmental Design (LEED) gold certification status in bronze on the first floor. However, as you maybe guessed quicker than I, this term had nothing to do with an environmental or ecological sense of "climate"—it was about race. Like the environment, which used to be outside, climate has now moved inside and is subject to various console controls in classrooms, labs, and offices. Along the way, it also became an effective managerial way of referencing race.

This usage nestles within pervasive academic, corporate, and political discourses that equate race with "diversity," a concept that was honed by ecologists and biologists in the 1970s to talk about the relative health of species. Diversity was crucial to the passage of the Endangered Species Act in 1973, and it informed subsequent biological discourses on the relative merits of "native" and "nonnative" species. By the 1980s, the term expanded in its reference to characterize humans as well. But not just any humans were diverse; *diversity* in managerial practices (from hiring decisions to "prejudice reduction workshops") refers to categories of people that might be required by law or for the sake of appearances to improve the profile of an institution, public or private. This is how it acquires racial connotations. Notably, it didn't stop referring to nonhumans when it was taken up in institutional discourses.

The initial critique of diversity discourse, in relation to race, is that it precluded an attention to power and history, especially at the institutional level. Chandra Mohanty diagnosed this years ago: "difference seen as benign variation (diversity), rather than as conflict, struggle, or the threat of disruption, bypasses power as well as history to suggest a harmonious, empty pluralism."[1] Mohanty marked this as the emergence of "the Race Industry, an industry that is responsible for the management, commodification, and *domestication of race* on American campuses."[2] It's an interesting formulation, this combined use of industry and domestication. Whereas diversity in ecology has subsequently led to efforts at "rewilding" the Great Plains and select corners of Europe, in social milieux, it generated industrial forms of domestication. Why the difference? But just as importantly, what of the similarities?

One way of answering the question is by considering whether the elision of power and history Mohanty critiqued pertains in the nonhuman domains of ecology, where *diversity* quickly morphed into *biodiversity,* a term E. O. Wilson honed to encourage humans to recognize and counteract the devastating impacts we've had on the planet (see "Have Culture, Will Travel"). Tentatively, I would say no, because ecological thought and discourse are rife with discussion of domination and power—"conflict," "disruption," "struggle"—and the inequalities they generate. Perhaps the inattention to power–history is the side effect of something else. Deborah Litvin suggested as much, naming, instead, "essentialism" and "categorical thinking" as the problem—one oft noted with race. She argued, "The importation of diversity from the bio-physical context of botanical and zoological taxonomy into the social-political context of the contemporary workplace has resulted in the portrayal of 'employee differences' as primarily a matter of category of membership."[3] This type of categorical sensibility is identified as inherent both in biological thought and in naturalizing ideological discourses. Perhaps that's correct.

The critique of diversity as a discourse of race today is articulated further by Sara Ahmed, who observes that "'diversity' is used as an adjective, as a way of describing the organization, a quality, or an attribute of an organization."[4] She points to the "paradox between, on the one hand, the routine use of the language of diversity by institutions and, on the other hand, the experience of many practitioners of an institutional resistance to diversity becoming routine." Her critique highlights capitalist discourse: "The shift to the language of diversity could thus be understood in market terms; diversity has commercial value and can be used as a way not only of marketing the university but of making the university into a marketplace."[5] I agree with all these points—that diversity discourse on humans deflects attention away from conflict and promotes a market-placed sensibility. But I doubt this is principally related to the term's biological connotations or derivation as a means of naturalizing race; it's the managerial rather than the natural shaping this "domestication" of race.

Ecological discourse, after all, has a ready place for power, conflict, and a critique of market rationality. As well, given the dynamics of speciation and hybridity—a botanical term that acquired great cachet in talking about race, favorably, though—typological thought is hardly a given of diversity discourse, either. The problem perhaps missed by these critiques is that the racial transpositions carry *very little understanding* of the biological realm along with them as they circulate. It's not too much biology but too little. This is compounded by the assumption that the trouble engendered by this circulation is that the biological is invoked at all in relation to the social. But what are we if not biological as well as cultural entities?

To pursue thinking culture across species lines, it matters very much to recognize that biology and culture are inseparable and that thinking the two together—as in biocultural approaches[6]—can be hugely generative for engaging racial discourses. In this sense, a limitation of these critiques is that they seek to foreclose an attention to that which potentially could disrupt the social discourse that makes race equivalent to "diversity." The trouble with "social Darwinism," after all, is twofold: that it is so detached from biology—inhibiting recognition of its plasticity, as with "artificial selection"—and that it badly underestimates the power of culture to shape both biology and genomes.[7] The bigger problem, as Mohanty initially identified, is the socialization of race: domesticating it and moving it indoors with the climate.[8] This critique should as easily run in the opposite direction: our inability to adequately address the social dynamics of race is leading to a misunderstanding of climate, making it increasingly difficult to talk about the "great outdoors."

Notes

1. Chandra Talpade Mohanty, "On Race and Voice: Challenges for Liberal Education in the 1990s," *Cultural Critique*, no. 14 (1989): 181.

2. Ibid., 186, emphasis added.

3. Deborah R. Litvin, "The Discourse of Diversity: From Biology to Management," *Organization* 4, no. 2 (1997): 203.

4. Sara Ahmed, *On Being Included: Racism and Diversity in Institutional Life* (Durham, N.C.: Duke University Press, 2012), 52.

5. Ibid., 52–53.

6. Kate Clancy, "I Can Out-Interdiscipline You: Anthropology and the Biocultural Approach," *Context and Variation* (blog), May 1, 2012, http://blogs.scientificamerican.com/context-and-variation/2012/05/01/biocultural-approach/.

7. Kevin N. Laland, John Odling-Smee, and Sean Myles, "How Culture Shaped the Human Genome: Bringing Genetics and the Human Sciences Together," *Nature Reviews Genetics* 11, no. 2 (2010): 137–48.

8. Sylvia Hurtado, "The Campus Racial Climate: Contexts of Conflict," *Journal of Higher Education* 63, no. 5 (1992): 539–69.

5

Horticultural Hermeneutic

In thinking critically about the circulation of terms like *diversity* and *native,* it is easy to focus on the role of metaphors—words that transpose one well-known domain of experience, transferring it, in a potentially explanatory sense, to the unfamiliar or unknown. But pointing out that certain metaphors, like *roots,* accompany racial thinking is not all that telling when what is operative here are not just tropes or the swerves of language but a deeper material conditioning of thought. What matters crucially is that underlying conditions of sameness make the apparent difference-breaching metaphorics quite sensible (see "Homology").

Consider, first, our utter dependence on plants; they make our existence possible. We rely on them for everything—food, energy, and the air we breathe. Not just we humans, either; the rise of mammals was predicated on the angiosperms' colonization of the globe. So how can we imagine that our seemingly unique capacity for thought and culture—from which are generated the collective representations that ensconce us within the social—is somehow entirely independent of this most crucial domain of the nonhuman? Not that we might think about this in a manner somehow free of metaphor; but before analyzing these tropes for the social or ideological operations they perform, we have to grasp how fully plants constitute the material predicates for our intelligence. The vestiges and contours of plants on our thinking are pervasive. If our thoughts and their objects take on a certain hew or configuration that seems to ground social orders in relation to natural objects—the ideological critique—this is because the *very basis for human intellection relies on plant life.*

In this sense, the horticultural hermeneutic is more than a set of metaphors; it's a figural frame of interlinking botanical elements: roots, fruits, seeds, trees, branches, even fields. The material-semiotic operation here may be more extensive than that Bruno Latour and Donna Haraway imagined, because not only do these material objects signify but our capacity to read their signification and render our own forms of it is physiologically dependent on these same items. The dependence is easily glimpsed within social theory, too, where highly active key terms like *hybrid*[1] and *contact zone*[2] come straight out of botany.[3]

These metaphorics are deeper than you might imagine. Take *semen*, for instance. With humans and other animals, this is a metaphoric extension of *seed*, which *stems* from a Latin *root*.[4] We figured out the seed's reproductive capacity and susceptibility to cultivation before we understood our own or that of our domesticated species. From bountiful references today to *roots* and *seeds*, to *branches* and *fruit*, a horticultural hermeneutic is clearly still operative: seed money for a tech startup company may be transferred through root directories and made accessible at a local bank branch. Computation and language, our two fundamental species accomplishments, are still principally comprehensible only through trees, their branches, and their stems—"tree languages" suggests their inexorable point of conflation. And not surprisingly, race is part of this entanglement, as linguist Thomas Bonfiglio demonstrates in *Mother Tongues and Nations*, where he traces the history of "arboreal madness" in European thought. "The organicizing of language in the service of nationalist interests contributed one of the most powerful metaphors to the conceptualization of language, that of the tree. What began as an attempt to valorize the vernacular by locating it in local organic nature and representing it as a phenomenon of botanical development would eventually generate abstract arboreal models of language. Moreover, this would also act to enracinate language, to frame it as a biological entity."[5] But is this the root of the problem with race, that language is organicized?

As with all things plant related, this all goes much deeper than race—or its antiquity suggests that this is an older form of thought than that associated with the "idea of race" (circa the Enlightenment). The contours of the horticultural hermeneutic—as with many Western interpretive frames—are on display in the Bible, where these botanical figures were deployed exactly to align the human reproductive capacity in relation to the reproduction of collectives, groups, kinds, or "nations."[6] For instance, "In days to come Jacob will take root, Israel will bud and blossom and fill all the world with fruit" (Isaiah 27:5–7). Or "Joseph is a fruitful vine, a fruitful vine near a spring, whose branches climb over a wall" (Genesis 49:22). In the New Testament, Jesus made prolific use of such figures, shifting from national patrimony to a more mystical register, as in "The good seed stands for the people of the kingdom" (Matthew 13:37–39). That this hermeneutic is central to how we understand racial and ethnic identities today is not just because it finds *fertile ground* in our imaginings of genes, biology, and language; rather, it's because all of these domains have been the subject of cultural operations for a good ten thousand years.

We glimpse this in Genesis 30:38–40: "Then he placed the peeled branches in all the watering troughs, so that they would be directly in front of the flocks when they came to drink. When the flocks were in heat and came to drink, they mated in front of the branches. And they bore young that were streaked or speckled or spotted. Jacob set apart the young of the flock by themselves, but made the rest face the streaked and dark-colored animals that belonged to Laban. Thus he made separate flocks for himself and did not put them with Laban's animals." This scene, with its elaborate concern with breeding distinct kinds, does not exclusively capture "Western thought." The Greek tradition, as developed later with Aesop's Fables, was more enamored of transspecies crossings of deities, humans, and nonhumans. Yet the integration of botany and breeding (in front of the peeled branches) indicates the antiquity of this predicament. Importantly, too, these objects or tropes are clearly not natural entities: these roots, seeds, and fruit are horticultural, the products of cultivation as well as nation and what we call today race.

More striking than the antiquity of this figural frame is both its consistency through the ages and its pervasive current deployment on the "frontiers" of knowledge in such *fields* as genomics and computational science. The more research advances, the more deeply embedded these figures become. Today it remains difficult to think language or analyze genetic structure without botanical forms. From the prevalence of dendrograms in computational biology—representing hierarchical clusterings of genes—or cladistics (from the Greek for "twig") and phylogenetic efforts to depict or detect most recent common ancestors (particularly in bioinformatics and systematics), figures of trees with their roots and branches, stems and nodes, are fundamental to both analysis and data productions. Phylogenetic analysis today proceeds on the same model Darwin suggested—a tree-shaped array of relations extending back through time, which he glimpsed via the figure of the "tree of life"[7]—one he then socialized by projecting of Victorian "genealogy" and capitalist "competition" onto nature.[8] In medicine, as well, the trope of "genetic roots," both for disease and for individual or collective forms of identity, is pervasive.[9] Now, what about the social aspect of all this?

Ideological analysis might well assert that these life-forms are being used to legitimate, rationalize, and reproduce social hierarchies and institutions. Fair enough. But consider that how we imagine the activities of genes and words is not just dependent on plant forms; these forms carry with them the very capacity to imagine the social—that is, the collective forms of distinctly shaped communicative patterns and phenotypes. The *root* organizes ideas about inheritance and social identity in a temporal sense associated with "kind"; the *seed* focuses thoughts not just on reproduction but on how that process is generative of forms of relatedness that link entities and organisms in a current moment; *flowers* permits postulates about communicative functions that link types and kinds, as perhaps best glimpsed in the development of floral grave linings that emerged even before domestication.[10] *Trees* combine each of these capacities, which is why sites of its metaphorical elaboration are useful opportunities for thinking socially across different life-forms. These are not just representations that project or "ground" the social; these form the basis for thought, even of how we formulate an analytic of the social. But this is hardly metaphoric; a basis of all this is that we share so much (genetically and culturally) in common with other life-forms.[11]

The analysis of metaphor typically focuses on distance and difference, from and between distinct objects. But what of the underlying forms of sameness that ground or generate the initial intuition that any two things may be connected this way? An important strand of the burgeoning research and theorizing on plants today strives to unthink the anthropocentric notions and conceits that keep us from recognizing intelligence and sentience in plants.[12] The basic insight—that people and plants are more alike than we realize—has long been simmering. Plant physiology—the recognition that they, too, comprise tissues, organs, and circulatory systems—emerged gradually in the late seventeenth century from a vast corpus of agricultural knowledge focused solely on utilitarian concerns.[13] Then Linnaeus formulated the "great analogy" by pointing out that plants, too, are sexual beings. Gregor Mendel's experiments with peas provoked a simultaneous recognition that we and they are genetic beings. The central insight keeps expanding, as best demonstrated in Daniel Chamovitz's research on the common sensory capacities—to see, feel, hear, and know—of humans and fauna.[14]

To deploy social analysis to identify and critique the operation of certain plant metaphors seems not as useful as asking how this broad metaphorics—the horticultural hermeneutic—opens onto underlying commonalities that are devilishly hard to glimpse from an the anthropomorphic mind-set, then, too, how these are also fundamental to our human capacity to imagine the social as well as cultural activities—language and computation, for instance—that we assume make us so unique. That horticultural metaphors abound today seems hardly as significant an observation as the question of why it has taken us so long to recognize fundamental forms of sameness that shaped this hermeneutic.

Notes

1. Homi K. Bhabha, "Cultural Diversity and Cultural Differences," in *The Post-colonial Studies Reader*, ed. B. Ashcroft, G. Griffiths, and H. Tiffin (New York: Routledge, 2006).

2. Mary Louise Pratt, "Arts of the Contact Zone," *Profession* (1991): 33–40.

3. See Pratt, "Arts of the Contact Zone," 33–40; Bhabha, "Cultural Diversity and Cultural Differences," 155–57.

4. "Ovaries," in contrast (and quite key in taxonomic identification), are considered as parallel *organs*. See "Homology."

5. Thomas Paul Bonfiglio, *Mother Tongues and Nations: The Invention of the Native Speaker* (Boston: De Gruyter, 2010), 94.

6. Carol Delaney, *The Seed and the Soil: Gender and Cosmology in Turkish Village Society* (Berkeley: University of California Press, 1991), shows how these figural forms also shape gender, with seed being equated with men and women with soil: "Seed and soil, seemingly such innocent images, condense powerful meanings: although they appear to go together naturally, they are categorically different, hierarchically ordered, and differentially valued. With seed, men appear to provide the creative spark of life, the essential identity of a child; while women, like soil, contribute the nurturant material that sustains it. This has been a predominant folk theory of procreation in the West for millennia" (8). But also see Haraway's account of the seed as a technoscientific figure (along with the chip, gene, fetus, brain, database, ecosystem, etc.): "a seed contains inside its coat the history of practices such as collecting, breeding, marketing, taxonomizing, patenting, biochemically analyzing, advertising, eating, cultivating, harvesting, celebrating, starving. A seed produced in the biotechnological institutions now spread around the world contains the specifications for labor systems, planning calendars, pest-control procedures, marketing, land holding, and beliefs about hunger and well-being." In Donna Haraway,
Modest_Witness@Second_Millennium.FemaleMan_Meets_OncoMouse: Feminism and Technoscience (New York: Routledge, 1997), 129; also 2, 11–12, 43, 89ff.

7. Helmreich, *Alien Ocean*.

8. See Marilyn Strathern, *After Nature: English Kinship in the Late Twentieth Century* (Cambridge: Cambridge University Press, 1992). Though Marx wanted to dedicate *Capital* to Darwin and was deeply drawn to his theory of evolution, he still read Darwin critically, as in a letter to Engels (June 18, 1862), remarking "how Darwin

recognizes among beasts and plants his English society, with its division of labor, competition, [and] opening up of markets."

9. "Global Genome Effort Seeks Genetic Roots of Disease," *ScienceDaily*, October 31, 2012, http://www.sciencedaily.com/releases/2012/10/121031141723.htm.

10. Jack Goody, *The Culture of Flowers* (Cambridge: Cambridge University Press, 1993).

11. In Kohn's multilayered discussion of thought across species lines, he notes that "form is difficult to treat anthropologically" and that "form requires us to rethink what we mean by the 'real.'" Kohn, *How Forests Think*, 20, 186. Succinctly, he asserts that "humans do not just impose form on the tropical forest; the forest proliferates it" (182). Also see his discussion of the "biosocial efficacy of forms" (167–68).

12. Craig Holdrege, *Thinking Like a Plant: A Living Science for Life* (Great Barrington, Mass.: Lindisfarne Books, 2013); Michael Marder, *Plant-Thinking: A Philosophy of Vegetal Life* (New York: Columbia University Press, 2013); Matthew Hall, *Plants as Persons: A Philosophical Botany* (Albany: State University of New York Press, 2011). Also see Natasha Myers's *Plant Studies Collaboratory*, http://plantstudies.wordpress.com/.

13. François Delaporte, *Nature's Second Kingdom: Explorations of Vegetality in the Eighteenth Century* (Cambridge, Mass.: MIT Press, 1982).

14. Daniel Chamovitz, *What a Plant Knows: A Field Guide to the Senses* (New York: Farrar, Straus, and Giroux, 2012).

6

Webs without Meaning

The core problem with social theory is that, in its emergence and its continued refinements, it insists on delineating culture from everything else. This is evident in any ideological analysis that asserts that what we're *really talking about* when we talk about nonhumans is just the social order, naturalizing the operations of domination and power. When we study, observe, or speculate about nonhumans, we are really talking about social hierarchies via a series of displacements or other Freudian tropes.

Eduardo Kohn frames this problem clearly, not surprisingly amid an inquiry that purposefully aims at "developing a more robust analytic for understanding human relations to nonhumans." Kohn asserts, "The fundamental belief that social science's greatest contribution—the recognition and delineation of a separate domain of socially constructed reality—is also its greatest curse."[1] The social constructionist stance revealed the ideological operations at work in naturalized notions of gender and race, in particular. But now it hinders us from ever talking or thinking—*really*—about anything other than human social orders. It creates a predicament whereby we imagine we can never escape from this cultural condition, or anthropocentrism. But anthropology has led the way in rejecting other "centrisms"—ethnocentrism, especially—and will do so again here, via the simple recognition or reminder that culture is not on only one side of a line between humans and nonhumans: *it's also and already on the other side.* Likely, our version of it came across that imaginary line, at some point in evolution, but most certainly our development of it as a concept that came to be applied exclusively to humans (for a while) drew extensively from engaging with and observing the nonhuman.

Cultural analysis, as we practice it today, is predicated on one of four ontologies that anthropologist Philippe Descola argues account for all humans' worldly orientations. People perceive, encounter, and know nonhuman species according to basic "schemas for integrating experience, which make it possible to structure, in a selective fashion, the flux of perception and relations." These schemas reflect "the same resources that every human carries within himself or herself: namely a body and intentionality." Of the four modes of identification—animism, totemism, analogism, and naturalism—"we Moderns" are ensconced within the latter.[2] We evoke "culture" or "society" as part of a schema of perception that uniquely "results in isolating the social domain as a separate regime of existence, with percepts that govern solely the sphere of human activity."[3] Whereas the other ontologies all feature projections of collectives that fundamentally encompass humans and nonhumans in a shared social order, naturalism is distinctive in making hard and fast distinctions between nature and culture, stipulating "that the treatment of humans and nonhumans stemmed from entirely separate mechanisms."[4] In this worldview, and especially "ever since Durkheim," cultural analysis is predicated on an insistence that phenomena are explainable "by the existence of particular social forms that were projected onto the world and modeled practices to objectivize the world and make it meaningful."[5] From this view, all glimpses of the natural world—from plant names to genus markers—are "social constructions," and people remain hermetically sealed in meaning-bound frames of reference, or "webs of significance."

The principal proponent of this view is Clifford Geertz; he spelled it out in his famous essay "Thick Description": "that man is an animal suspended in webs of significance he himself has spun, I take culture to be those webs."[6] But of course, humans don't spin webs; spiders do. That this foundational statement on culture as meaning relies on a metaphorical leap across species boundaries suggests the impossibility of ever fully or uniquely equating culture with "Man." More importantly, this is a reminder that *the usage of "culture" on humans is metaphorical;* the word's original, "concrete" meaning had to do with plants and soil. This meaning endures and is quite widespread, as Hannah Landecker relates in her lab-based ethnography *Culturing Life: How Cells Became Technologies.*[7]

Juxtapose this material version of culture-as-propagative-medium with Geertz's further elaboration, in that same essay, of the "semiotic concept of culture and an interpretive approach to the study of it."[8] He figures it through an Indian story, told to an Englishman, that the world rests on the back of a turtle, who rests on the back of another turtle; below that, "it is turtles all the way down." Cultural analysis goes astray, Geertz contended, when it goes "in search of all-too-deep-lying turtles."[9] Donna Haraway eschews this concern and takes this fable literally, while also taking up this risk, by invoking biological research on turtles that reveals how "reciprocal induction within and between always-in-process critters ramifies through space and time on both large and small scales in cascades of inter- and intra-action."[10] Through such recursive shifts in scale and scope, Haraway concludes that "companion-species worlds are turtles all the way down." Leaving meaning behind at the "surface" of humanity, such encultured relations extend what we can recognize as culture. In the mud below meaning,[11] we find intraspecies dynamics of mutualism that may offer the very basis for sociality and that certainly leads, for some species, to cultivation, as addressed in the next foray (see "What Is a Garden?").

Returning to the metaphorics of webs and meaning, though, aligning spiders and people offer another literally minded set of lessons regarding sociality. This starts with the fact that some species of spiders are, like us, social. Not many are—only some twenty-five out of more than thirty-nine thousand known species. But these engage in behaviors that humans do too: caring for each other's offspring, cooperating in assailing prey, and sharing food. Similar to eusocial species—bees, ants, and wasps—they swarm and live in colonies, pursuing cooperative nest maintenance, but whether they have defined castes is somewhat unclear. At another level, as initial DNA sequencing data are being produced, surprising glimpses emerge of genomic parallels with humans. "The first genome sequence of the araneomorph velvet spider and a fragmented genome sequence of the mygalomorph tarantula" found that the "structure of the spider genome, unlike other arthropod genomes, is characterized by short exons and long introns very similar to the human genome."[12] This homology was unexpected; researchers were looking to understand how spiders' abilities to produce silk and venom could be turned toward industrial uses, as in biomaterials, pesticides, and medicine.

More provocatively, though, social spiders are perhaps emerging as model organisms (see "Model Organisms") for studying personality. Natalie Angier reports in the *New York Times* on this trend: "The new work on social spiders is part of the expanding field of animal personalities research, which seeks to delineate, quantify, and understand the many stylistic differences that have been identified in a vast array of species, including monkeys, minks, bighorn sheep, dumpling squid, zebra finches and spotted hyenas."[13] The key finding—that "personality is powerfully influenced by the other spiders in the group"—echoes one made by Claude Lévi-Strauss in *The Savage Mind*: "social life effects a strange transformation . . . , for it encourages each biological individual to develop a personality." From this effect, "everything takes place as if in our civilization every individual's own personality were his own totem: it is a signifier of his signified being."[14] Angier notes, "spiders in a stable social setting grew less like one another over time"; "far from fostering behavioral conformity, a predictable social life accentuated each spider's quirks and personal style, rather as characters in a sitcom."[15]

A social theorist might start with that last line and assail every aspect of this paralleling, from the quantification of "boldness" and "timidity" to the very interest in "character building"; from the disciplinary suppositions of the psychological science of "personality development" to the biopolitical interests that likely influence the funding for such studies. But perhaps the most fraught are the elements that return us to the very bases for thinking of and mobilizing the social in an analytical frame this way. Channeling Durkheim, "the spider communities gain their strength through a division of labor, with some members specializing in web repair, some in attacking or subduing pretty."[16] Echoing Weber, "yet the process of finding one's true spider calling is a gradual one, and depends on an assessment of the needs of the larger spider society."[17] This should make spiders as interesting for their social and genomic parallels to humans as for their metaphorical potential to model our meaning-bound predicament, especially when "the spider work neatly illustrates the mix of plasticity and predilection that underlies personality."[18] Are the ideological aspects—meaning in the service of power—much more telling than the intriguing parallel versions of sociality that spiders present?

Notes

1.   Kohn, *How Forests Think*, 7.

2.   Philippe Descola, *Beyond Nature and Culture* (Chicago: University of Chicago Press, 2013), 232–33.

3.   Ibid., 247.

4.   Ibid., 248.

5.   Ibid., 124.

6.   Clifford Geertz, *The Interpretation of Cultures* (New York: Basic Books, 1973), 5.

7. Hannah Landecker, *Culturing Life: How Cells Became Technologies* (Cambridge, Mass.: Harvard University Press, 2010).

8. Geertz, *Interpretation of Cultures*, 29.

9. Ibid., 30.

10. Donna Haraway, *When Species Meet* (Minneapolis: University of Minnesota Press, 2007), 32.

11. See Stuart McLean, "Black Goo: Forceful Encounters with Matter in Europe's Muddy Margins," *Cultural Anthropology* 26, no. 4 (2012): 589–619, and Helmreich, *Alien Ocean*.

12. Kristian W. Sanggaard, Jesper S. Bechsgaard, Xiaodong Fang, Jinjie Duan, Thomas F. Dyrlund, Vikas Gupta, Xuanting Jiang, et al., "Spider Genomes Provide Insight into Composition and Evolution of Venom and Silk," *Nature Communications* 5 (2014): 2.

13. Natalie Angier, "The Lives of Sociable Spiders," *New York Times*, May 13, 2014.

14. Claude Lévi-Strauss, *The Savage Mind* (London: Weidenfeld and Nicolson, 1966), 214.

15. Angier, "Sociable Spiders."

16. Ibid.

17. Ibid.

18. Ibid.

7

What Is a Garden?

In *The Wild Life of Our Bodies,* biologist Rob Dunn characterizes the appendix as "a Zen garden of microbial life."[1] This metaphor arises in his discussion of changing medical views about this strange organ's function—how doctors shifted from viewing this "dangly bit of flesh that hangs from the lower intestine" as a "simply antiqued, useless vestigial organ" to considering that it importantly shelters bacteria, apart "from the wash and grind of the intestines themselves."[2] Overturning centuries of disregard for the appendix (since removing it seemed to produce no ill effects), this recent notion also upends a long-standing view about health and illness: "For most of the history of human medicine," Dunn explains, "we have thought of other species as negative. Bacteria kill us. Fungi kill us."[3] This view of appendix-as-garden takes in a recognition of our mutualism with species of bacteria—specifically that "the good bacteria of the intestine" have to be sheltered against the onslaught caused by pathogens such as cholera. A "garden," though—and a Zen one at that? Is there another way of framing or articulating this perception? For that matter, is it fair to say that our bodies may be cultivating the bacteria on which we are dependent? Could "we," as individual selves, play a purposeful role in that cultivation?

Dunn doesn't come by this use of "garden" haphazardly. It arises because he was just, in the previous chapter, writing about ants. And he was doing so for the common reasons science writers turn to ants, generally: they offer intriguing, complex parallels with humans. In particular, Dunn was trying to get some perspective on us humans, and doing so comparatively, in juxtaposition with ants, by also considering the role of IgA antibodies. "Our body is not unlike an ant nest, composed of multiple cells and multiple species."[4] If we can recognize that the existence of ants in these nests is dependent on a "complex microbial slew," can we see the same is true of our bodies? "The appendix is a window into our similarity to the ants and other life-forms."[5] This similarity, though, is *not just about mutualism but rather its cultivated forms*. The intuition that glimpses this is dependent on a series of parallels: "To really see what is going on, one needs to step back far enough to see parallels, the reverberating similarities between one field or organism and another." In this view, "farming ants are more like us than any other species."[6] He grounds this claim with a quick survey of research on leaf-cutter ant colonies, which contain gardens of fungi. He relates, then, that "the idea that our bodies might farm good microbes, for our defense, came first from the ants."[7] Here he is specifically referencing the work of biologist Cameron Currie, but he stresses the point that this idea—this thought or intuition—arises from nonhumans. For it to be realized and developed, though, depends on countering anthropocentric sensibilities about the uniqueness, sophistication, and superiority of our species, especially in contrast to an emblem of insignificance—the ant. To achieve this opening, Dunn asserts, "We are more like a leaf-cutter ant colony than anyone had imagined, in terms of how we tend our microbial gardens."[8]

Is this usage of *garden* metaphorical? Answering yes assumes that the original, literal meanings of the term are associated with the human practices and locus and also that the real object of gardening is plants. Working backward, here, the more we learn about plants, the more we recognize that they depend on microbial "layerings of turtles," too.[9] More importantly, ants have been doing both—cultivating microbes and gardens—for hundreds of millions of years. As with "culture," we humans are late to the game and probably should consider that there is little anthropomorphism in extending "gardening" to ants' activities, if they came up with it first. The gain here, though, is not just recognizing gardens as a homologous form but revamping and reconsidering what the acts and objects of gardening entail or encompass. Yes, microbes can be objects of gardening, as is increasingly promoted as a means to shift the metaphorical language around the human gut away from the warfare model and toward something less hostile.[10] There quickly follows a renewed attention to "cultivation": here we see the process that produces culture not only working homologously, in ants and humans, but in doing so, exactly entangling multiple species, perhaps most impressively in the rainforests of Peru, where ants—*Duroia hirsuta*—tend "devil's gardens" of single tree species by controlling vegetation through pruning or poisoning other species.[11]

From gardening to cultivation, we begin to hone in on what might be the *core features of culture* that we can use to identify across species. In this version, it is not meaning that matters so much as the capacity to care for—to domesticate—other species: to render them plastic and mutable rather than the fixed types we often imagine natural objects to be. From culture—that which many sociable nonhumans might possess—to cultivation, which entails some form of division of labor with the capacity to transform and enlist other species, we achieve a shift in scale of relating and relationships. From the variety of multispecies relations to study, cultivation stands out as warranting greater attention, and culture is requisite to understanding this mutually informing dynamic. Like domestication, cultivation involves questions of who's doing what to whom. They're both about, or largely assumed to entail, conscious, volitional acts. But the more we consider each, the greater the possibilities seem of unconscious and unintentional developments. They're entangled in important narratives and assumptions about the emergence of contemporary humanity, each touching in different ways on "culture": domestication as that thing which our capacity for culture allowed us to pursue; cultivation, overlapping with this connotation, but also standing as the perhaps originary drive from which culture emerged. Both are inflections of lines between wild (lacking in humanity) and civilized (the epitome of civilization). Both involve that key doubling term, *breeding*, as noun and verb.

Because cultivation leads directly to culture, this is where the possibilities of thinking and writing simultaneously about humans and nonhumans crystalize. Yes, maybe the human is shot through with multispecies, on which our very existence depends,[12] but can they do what we do when we cultivate? Clearly only a few species can—an even smaller number, by far, than we characterize as "social." Gardens and their presence in the operations of certain species offer an initial opening to consider this larger issue. There are few more overdetermined, oft invoked figures than the garden, the mythic–real space where people begin, as in the Garden of Eden. Yet doesn't the meaning-bearing aspect of gardens sheer off when they are construed as a homology? If we can settle on nonhuman forms of gardens and gardening, then it becomes easier to think about cultivation and culture as a transspecies homology.

But where would all this end? If ants garden, do they also build highways and organize market economies? The homologues between ants and humans are copious, such that they raise the question of where such intuitions or metaphors obscure more than they reveal, or when their ideological function predominates, such that the portraiture becomes more about humans than about ants. Numerous versions of fables concerning the industriousness of ants indicate that there has been a practically limitless interest in aligning ants and people in a comparative frame directed toward exhortations to work harder and be more cooperative. Where does the shift occur from homologue to myth? Consider the work of ecologist Mark Moffatt, and especially his book *Adventures among Ants*. He writes, "The commonalities between ants and people are striking. Both alter nature and build nurseries, fortresses, stockyards, and highways, while nurturing friends and livestock and obliterating enemies and vermin. Both ants and humans express tribal bonds and basic needs through ancient and elaborate codes. Both create universes of their own devising through the scale of their domination of the environment."[13] Obviously, this is a seductive perspective—and one that is deeply troubling, because the parallels very quickly scale up to the operation of power and dominance in society. It's not just that this comparative frame yields up a plethora of naturalistic renditions of a market economy: ant scouts, for instance, "hawk their merchandise by regurgitating samples into the mouths of 'buyers' in the nest chambers"; "if the buyers find their 'customers' have become sated," and so on.[14] Moffatt's use of scare quotes suggests he is either cautious or circumspect about such analogies, though not so much when noting that "many species use child labor"[15] or when referring to slavery and "virtual police states."[16] The bigger problem seems to arise when the ants appear to be better than us in organizing their society.

Moffatt extols that "their smoothly run societies make ours, marred by meddling, sharp differences of opinion, cheating, selfishness, outright aggression, and occasional homicides, look positively dysfunctional."[17] Social theorists would quickly dice up this claim to make the point that such analogies consistently run one way: idealizing a perfect social order that can only be attained by dictatorial dominance. As such, social theory remains an important companion in this trajectory of thought, because it reminds us of the work and significance of ideology—a force that may well separate us in consequential ways from other eusocial species. But Moffatt's account is not reducible to these speculations on how ants can model a better society for humans. Importantly, there is something profoundly excessive in such comparison that leads perhaps as powerfully to a recognition of the need to rethink our basic concepts and fundamental categories. Moffatt notes that "supercolonies confound our notions about societies, populations, and species like nothing else."[18] If these concepts can be rendered unmoored and fluid, then it is much harder to link a series of parallels to claims about how society should be. This is the potential that lies, tenuously, in thinking about gardens across species lines.

Notes

1. Rob Dunn, *The Wild Life of Our Bodies: Predators, Parasites, and Partners That Shape Who We Are Today* (New York: Harper, 2011), 104.

2. Ibid., 93–94, 98.

3. Ibid., 105.

4. Ibid., 107.

5. Ibid.

6. Ibid., 87.

7. Ibid., 89.

8. Ibid., 90.

9. Haraway, *When Species Meet.*

10. Carl Zimmer, "Tending the Body's Microbial Garden," *New York Times*, June 18, 2012; Michael Pollan, "Some of My Best Friends Are Germs," *New York Times*, May 15, 2013.

11. Andreas Von Bubnoff, "Ants Make 'Devil's Garden' of Eden," *Nature News*, September 2005.

12. Dorion Sagan, *Cosmic Apprentice: Dispatches from the Edges of Science* (Minneapolis: University of Minnesota Press, 2013).

13. Mark W. Moffett, *Adventures among Ants: A Global Safari with a Cast of Trillions* (Berkeley: University of California Press, 2011), 223.

14. Ibid., 120.

15. Ibid., 118.

16. Ibid., 228.

17. Ibid., 216.

18. Ibid., 218.

8

Homology

Homology is a basis for considering forms of sameness across species; it frames the capacity and desire to think comparatively about life-forms and to learn from their commonalities. The idea is simple: an underlying continuity, based on common descent, generates similar structures in distinct species. "Structures" here principally means morphological features and refers predominantly to organs or bodily forms: traits. These might also arise similarly in species that don't share common ancestors; this is homoplasy, generated from convergent or parallel evolutionary trajectories in interactions with similar environments. Unlike metaphor, these recognitions are neither lyric nor figurative. They derive from shared evolutionary trajectories. Similar to the early history of anthropology, though, homology and homoplasy are conceptually organized by delineating structure and function. Whereas cultural anthropologists temporarily resolved this opposition with "structural-functionalism"—until the "cultural turn" shifted attention to conflict and meaning—biologists steadfastly kept the two separate. Hence, "analogy" (or "homoplasy" or "homoplastic") is commonly used for traits that may function similarly irrespective of structural dimensions. Perhaps not surprisingly, behavior—not as easily delineated as organs or traits and also of interest to cultural anthropologists—remains somewhat challenging to construe in terms of homology.

The significance of homology has been characterized by what it reveals about evolution, but might it also tell us about culture—culture, here, being the name for the dynamic or domain that operates on evolution, channeling gene flows in socially conventional directions? If evolution is about the mutation of genes and descent with modification, culture marks the point where that genetic process is no longer entirely "natural" (as in "natural selection"), where the heritable and nonheritable are combined in a socially transmissible form across generations. But because culture might also evolve,[1] this all gets complicated quickly, which brings us back to behavior.[2]

Drew Rendall, an evolutionary biologist, and Anthony Di Fiore, a physical anthropologist, argue for including behavior—"the totality of an animal's ways of interacting with its physical and social environments"[3]—within the gamut of homology. Behaviors "such as mating, dispersal, parental care, spatial navigation, range use, migration, and territorial defense are not easily connected to structural underpinnings and are best characterized only in functional terms."[4] These behaviors may be *both* cultural and evolutionary—that is, shaped by selection, artificial and/or natural. Sorting this out, though, "raises the bedeviling problems of how to characterize the relationship between an organism, its behavior and morphology, and the environment."[5] Rendall and Di Fiore aim largely to show that behavior can as readily register and respond to selection pressures as do morphological traits; hence their discussion turns to "*ethospecies*—species distinguishable only on the basis of behavioral differences"[6]—and epigenetics.[7] But their effort at coaxing or framing an emerging consensus on viewing potentially social activities as homologues is also a useful means for social theorists to think about cultural forms across species lines.

Currently the concept of homology—systematic similarities of relative positions in different orders—is very limited in cultural anthropology.[8] It could be used far more to frame and consider comparable forms of sociality across species lines. But this potential usage perhaps remains somewhat stunted by Lévi-Strauss's deployment of it in an effort to align mythical forms with ritual practices or elaborations.[9] When Gilles Deleuze and Felix Guattari discussed the concept in relation to structuralism, it was largely to dismiss it in favor of the acts of imagination required to recognize forms of becoming, specifically "becoming-animal" forms that may not be nameable yet. This discussion arose from their reflection on "the problem of natural history"—a concern with resemblances among life-forms that preceded evolutionary thought.[10] Their account turns on an assertion that analogies—of series or structure—should not be ceded strictly to the authority or domain of science:

For, on the one hand, the relationships between animals are the object not only of science but also of dreams, symbolism, art and poetry, practice and practical use. And on the other hand, the relationships between animals are bound up with the relations between man and animal, man and woman, man and child, man and the elements, man and the physical and microphysical universe. The twofold idea 'series-structure' crosses a scientific threshold at a certain moment; but it did not start there and it does not stay there, or else crosses over into other sciences, animating, for example, the human sciences, serving in the study of dreams, myths, and organizations.[11]

Indeed, their account is a condemnation of Lévi-Strauss for diminishing this intuition by driving it firmly back across the threshold of science in his discussion of totemism, which they summarize as follows: "The animal is distributed according to differential relations or distinctive oppositions between species; the same goes for human beings, according to the groups considered. When analyzing the institution of the totem, we do not say that this group of people identifies with that animal species. We say that what group A is to group B, species A is to species B"; thus "metamorphoses of the imagination" are supplanted "with conceptual metaphors."[12] Interestingly, they treat homology somewhat more favorably regarding the work of Étienne Geoffroy St. Hilaire (1772–1844), a French naturalist intrigued by the transmutation of species in time; his son, Isidore, would go on to found ethology. Deleuze and Guattari construe him as envisioning "a fixed plane of life upon which everything stirs, slows down or accelerates. A single abstract Animal for all the assemblages that effectuate it. A unique plane of consistency or composition."[13] They intone, "We must try to conceive of this world in which a single fixed plane—which we shall call a plane of absolute immobility or absolute movement—is traversed by nonformal elements of relative speed that enter this or that individuated assemblage depending on their degrees of speed and slowness."[14] They further imagine this as "a plane of consistency occupied by an immense abstract machine comprising an infinite number of assemblages."[15]

Their effort at a leveling perception of life-forms is ontological and concerned with becomings, with transformative possibilities for all life-forms. And as homology, from St. Hilaire, spills over into evolutionary thought with its classificatory, taxonomic fixations, they turn away: "Society and the State need animal characteristics to use for classifying people; natural history and science need characteristics in order to classify the animals themselves."[16] Instead, "we are not interested in characteristics; what interests us are modes of expansion, propagation, occupation, contagion, peopling."[17] But as much as they resist the social here—as an analytical frame or object of focus—it's interesting that the animals they are drawn to are exactly social ones: pack animals, specifically. Their gesture is broad: "A becoming-animal always involves a pack, a band, a population, a peopling, in short, a multiplicity."[18] But it hinges on the characteristic of "pack," even though they disavow any taxonomic schematizing. "What we are saying is that every animal is fundamentally a band, a pack.

That it has pack modes, rather than characteristics, even if further distinctions within these modes are called for. It is at this point that the human being encounters the animal."[19] Or, this may be rephrased: the point when people are ready to engage in recognition across a symbolic boundary avidly policed by many political, legal, and philosophical interests is directed toward distinctly social entities—human and nonhuman. Then culture comes into view again, from across this boundary, warranting greater attention.

In crossing this line, in thinking about similarities between and among species as they pertain to sociality, homology opens up conceptually. Deleuze and Guattari turn away from homology because they see in Lévi-Strauss's usage a term that only insulates the human within its supposedly unique sphere of sociality. Homologies are colonized, constrained, and construed as ideological operations, projections, or mere anthropomorphisms. But drawing on the concept's career—both in biology and before it crossed the "scientific threshold"[20]—suggests, contrarily, that homologies are more than social constructions; they identify commonalities that undercut a strict delineation of the human and nonhuman, as indicated by comparative genomics. As these commonalities extend beyond the strictly evolutionary into the forms that are shaped socially, the capacity to think in terms of and to deploy homology opens up the potential of breaching the insistence on humans as inescapably ensconced in a hermetically sealed domain of culture.

But if behaviors generally—in their heritable and nonheritable forms—still represent a challenge for thinking in terms of homology, how much more difficult would it be to consider culture in this frame? Specifically, how are we to think about the homologous forms of culture across species lines when culture is a force with the capacity to shape and direct evolution? Will this use of homology be principally characterized by sameness or by genealogy/ancestry and "communities of descent"?[21] This brings us back to the *Origin of the Species*, where Darwin laid out the case for recognizing natural selection by first depicting its cultural versions, "artificial selection." These life-forms he deployed were all, by definition, domesticated species. Did their domestication, as with Deleuze and Guattari's "becoming-animal," depend on or reach out to established, nonhuman forms of sociality? Pursuing culture across species lines may hinge on this question (see "Domestication").

Notes

1. Whitten et al., "Culture Evolves."

2. Homology entails an attention to a variety of "levels" or scales in biology, from the structural (embryonic development or epigenetic processes) to the behavioral to the genetic. At each level, questions of its scope, focus, and referents are considerable. At the genetic, for instance, does it pertain to the same genes (whether in different animals or not), the same genes with similar or different function, or similar genetic networks? See Alec L. Panchen, "Homology—History of a Concept," in *Homology*, ed. Gregory R. Bock and Gail Cardew, 5–23 (New York: John Wiley, 1999).

3. Drew Rendall and Anthony Di Fiore, "Homoplasy, Homology, and the Perceived Special Status of Behavior in Evolution," *Journal of Human Evolution* 52 (2007): 504.

4. Ibid., 507.

5. Ibid., 511.

6. Ibid.

7. Ibid., 512.

8. A search of *Anthrosource* turns up only one reference to "homology" (in 1985) and six for "homologous," as in the following: "The notion of cosmic intersubjectivity allows us to understand how the whole universe is considered to be a living being, materialized through a variety of sacred instruments." Robin M. Wright, "Fixed Forms and Fluid Powers: Intersubjective Cosmos and Personhood," *Anthropology and Humanism* 37, no. 2 (2012): 156–76.

9. Lévi-Strauss used homology to talk about difference rather than sameness, but in "parallel series." In relation to "so-called totemic institutions," Lévi-Strauss explained, "The homology they evoke is not between social groups and natural species but between the differences which manifest themselves on the level of groups on the one hand and on that of species on the other. They are thus based on the postulate of a homology between two systems of differences, one of which occurs in nature and the other in culture." Lévi-Strauss, *Savage Mind*, 115; see also 80, 172, 224–27.

10. See, first, Michel Foucault, *The Order of Things: An Archaeology of Human Sciences* (1972; repr., New York: Random House, 2012); then Alberto Corsín Jiménez, *An Anthropological Trompe L'oeil for a Common World: An Essay on the Economy of Knowledge* (New York: Berghahn Books, 2013).

11. Gilles Deleuze and Félix Guattari, *A Thousand Plateaus: Capitalism and Schizophrenia* (Minneapolis: University of Minnesota Press, 1987), 235.

12. Ibid., 257–58.

13. Ibid., 255.

14. Ibid.

15. Ibid., 256.

16. Ibid., 239.

17. Ibid.

18. Ibid.

19. Ibid.

20. See the range of discussions that reengage philosopher Johann Wolfgang von Goethe's *Metamorphosis of Plants* (1790), such as "From Leaf to Flower: Revisiting Goethe's Concepts on the 'Metamorphosis' of Plants, Marcel Carnier Dornelas and Odair Dornelas," *Brazilian Journal of Plant Physiology* 17, no. 4 (2005): 335–43, and Gordon Miller's critical introduction to his translation of Goethe's *The Metamorphosis of Plants* (Cambridge, Mass.: MIT Press, 2009).

21. Homology remains differentiated from analogy or homoplasy by an emphasis, following Darwin, on the study of genealogical relationships. But given that Darwin projected "genealogy" onto "nature," this is hardly a neutral or given set of "facts of evolution." Biologist David B. Wake laments of the enduring confusion over this term: "We have taken an ancient term, accepted it as real, and then reified it to serve our purposes." Wake, "Homoplasy, Homology, and the Problem of 'Sameness' in Biology," *Homology* (1999): 26.

9

Species Thinking

Dipesh Chakrabarty uses the phrase "species thinking" to characterize a major twist in social theory. This is a mode of thinking that takes humanity-as-species for its object: a shift from the condition of "species being" as invoked by Marx toward an analytic awareness based on a recognition of "boundary parameters of human existence."[1] For an historian and critic of globalization—that earth-encompassing phenomenon, feeding on and reproducing inequality wherever it travels—this is a notable shift in focus for Chakrabarty, because it entails thinking humanity in "universal" terms. He elaborates, "These parameters are independent of capitalism. . . . They have been stable for much longer than the histories of [its] institutions."[2] These parameters come into view out of a breach "between the present historiography of globalization and the historiography demanded by *anthropogenic theories of climate change.*"[3]

Species, he acknowledges, "is a word that will never occur in any standard history or political-economic analysis of globalization." In contrast, species thinking "is connected to the enterprise of *deep history*"[4] or the Anthropocene—the idea that humanity has impacted the planet in such a thoroughgoing manner as to constitute a distinct, new geological era. Revoicing Walter Benjamin, he suggests that "species may indeed be the name of a placeholder for an emergent, new universal history of humans that flashes up in the moment of danger that is climate change." In this precarious moment, the power–history frame of social theory proves singularly inadequate: the "critique that sees humanity as an effect of power" is insufficient "in dealing with the crisis of global warming."[5] In this view, a cultural analysis limited to assessing the "social conditions of possibility" of an idea or life-form—privileging capital and politics (e.g., "neoliberalism"), reinscribing or delimiting the social as a uniquely human—reproduces anthropocentrism and is insufficient for grasping our species's predicament.

For a species that has given a good deal of thought to species,

Chakrabarty's concept is a notable development. The fact that species are "good to think" provided the basis for articulating sociality for perhaps as long as humans formed into durable group arrangements. As well, this theoretical formulation crucially opened an enormous intellectual capacity to recognize logical or analytical thought operating on and through a variety of nonhumans, while leveling the hierarchical contrast between civilized and primitive thought. Strikingly, the recognition of species being was also central for the transformation of social theorizing with Marx. In the *Economic and Philosophical Manuscripts,* Marx declared, "In the mode of life activity lies the entire character of a species, its species-character, and free conscious activity is the species-character of man"[6]—that odd species that bears the history making capacity to transform "life itself."

Markedly underscoring the fundamentally social orientation of this concept, species thinking arises out of an analytical intuition rather than a phenomenological sensibility. That's because, in Chakrabarty's formulation, it is not possible to grasp species thinking experientially: "We humans never experience ourselves as a species. . . . There could be no phenomenology of us as a species . . . no one ever experiences being a concept."[7] This arguably matches the central tenet of biological thought: that natural selection works on the individual rather than the species; the phenomenological experience of species being is continually forestalled by the operation of "selective pressures" on individual, competitive, reproductive units—but if not phenomenologically, then through our capacity to recognize both culture generally and its similar operations among other species. For the very recognition of this moment of peril is linked to the fact of the transformative efficacy of the Anthropocene to raise "artificial selection" onto a competitive plane with its "natural" counterpart.

This mode of thinking requires two analytical developments: (1) abstracting out the "human" as defined by a set of parameters (an historical process tracked by Michel Foucault, via the concept of population) and (2) recognizing that our species being is paralleled in other species, shifting reflections on these other collective life-forms away from ways of principally articulating and inscribing social difference (totemisms/ideology). The oft disparaged naturalism that characterizes the ontological orientation of "Westerners" is crucial in this development and marks a strategic resource in how social theory is developed and deployed. The challenge of not succumbing to "social Darwinist" misreadings of Darwin and misunderstandings of evolution lies exactly in recognizing the centrality of "artificial selection"—the actions of culture and cultivation—in leading people to see, first, parallel natural operations and, second, humanity's leveled place alongside all other life-forms. More on this second development later (see "Domestication"). First, let's turn to Foucault.

Foucault recognized this capacity for abstracting out the human-as-species developing at a particular moment, when biopower and biopolitics emerged in Europe in the 1600s. As he narrates in *The History of Sexuality, Volume One,* "Western man was gradually learning what it meant to be a living species in a living world, to have a body, conditions of existence, probabilities of life, an individual and collective welfare, forces that could be modified, and a space in which they could be distributed in an optimal manner."[8] This was made possible through the generation and analysis of increasing amounts of data on life and death, compiled by the State. Social theorists are well versed in this narrative, but it warrants quick review: "power is situated and exercised at the level of life, the species, the race, and the large-scale phenomena of population."[9] What draws somewhat less attention is the central role played by agriculture, both in this historical development and in Foucault's formulation of these key concepts. Where famines—as with epidemics and war—had previously been a constant threat and limit to humanity, "the improvement of agricultural techniques" opened this new possibility to alter "the pressure exerted by the biological on the historical."[10] That is, extending forms of cultivation were crucial to the "biopolitics of population."

In *Security, Territory, Population,* Foucault relates how the latter term acquired its modern meaning. "Population" was linked fundamentally to *depopulation,* the effects of military slaughter of humans and the ravaging of grain crops that induced famine and starvation during the Thirty Year War.[11] In much the way *populate* is used today as a verb in relation to databases and websites, the term focused on governments' need to extend forms of cultivation in support of new congeries of humans in territories that had been emptied of both. Foucault writes, "The problem of population was raised . . . in an essentially negative way. What was called the population was basically the contrary of depopulation. That is to say, 'population' was understood as the movement by which a deserted territory was repopulated after a great disaster, be it an epidemic, war, or food shortage, after one of these great dramatic moments in which people died with spectacular rapidity and intensity. Let's say that the problem of population was posed in relation to the desert or desertification due to major human catastrophe"[12]—a formulation that aligns closely with our current attention to the Anthropocene as a human-induced desertifica tion of the planet—when a "moment of danger," flashing up, gives us the species in relief, recognized fleeting in its anticipated absence.

This glimpse is not far different from the initial intuition of species, which both Chakrabarty and Foucault concur entails an epistemological rather than a phenomenological recognition. As Foucault recounts, "The dimension in which the population is immersed amongst other living beings appears and is sanctioned when, for the first time, men are no longer called 'mankind' and begin to be called 'the human species.' With the emergence of mankind as a species, within a field of the definition of all living species, we can say that man appears in the first form of his integration within biology. *From one direction, then, population is the human species, and from another it is what will be called the public.*"[13] *Population*, like *native* and *cosmopolitan*, opens up the capacity not just to see the human species but to begin to pursue the broader gamut of "species thinking." Continuing with Foucault's account: "*The population is therefore everything that extends from biological rootedness through the species up to the surface that gives one a hold provided by the public. From the species to the public*; we have here a whole field of new realities in the sense that they are the pertinent elements for mechanisms of power, the pertinent space within which and regarding which one must act."[14]

While *population* takes us "from the species to the public," it also takes us across the line between the human and nonhuman. As with *indigenous* or *native*, but with a far greater range, *population* levels and equates that which constitutes us with that which constitutes them, largely because of underlying sameness stemming from the genetic realm. Foucault's concern was principally the entry of nature into history and the field of power; but he was aware of another direction of thought that opened here, turning away from the figure of the human species that was coming into greater relief as a life-form with certain biological predicates and parameters. This was Darwin and the leveling of our life-form alongside that of all others. Genetics fulfilled this intuition and relied heavily on the concept of population in doing so. As Foucault observed, "Darwin found that population was the medium between the milieu and the organism, with all the specific effects of population: mutations, eliminations, and so forth. So in the analysis of living beings it is the transition from natural history to biology."[15] And then, again, from biology to social theory.

For biologists, the career and contours of *population* are slightly different. Analytically, population is both a generic, abstract container for variation—the raw material of natural selection—and an evolutionary entity, "an interbreeding community of organisms that share in an evolutionary process."[16] In the first version, it is an aggregation comprising entirely "individuals," whereas the second conceptualization is concerned with a group or collectives, "community" as Darwin used the term, "*community of species*" and "*community of descent.*" Following Mendel's experiments in breeding, this latter set of connotations around population attains its modern cast. As geneticist Jody Hey explains, "for the early geneticists, the idea of a random mating population was a theoretical breakthrough that allowed them to envision what Mendel's laws might mean for the frequencies of inherited traits in nature, outside of the laboratory and garden."[17] But if "random" equates to "natural selection"—unmotivated, undirected, mutations and their reproduction—"culture" must kick in when something like "mating" becomes nonrandom, among humans and our domesticates certainly, but potentially among other social species. But is this yet "breeding"? With species thinking, we don't escape the allegorical tendencies potentially influencing any reflection on nonhumans or the mind-set that finds them "good to think" in arranging, speculating on, and reproducing social identities and arrangements. But we open the potential to do so, to shift from an anxiety over the culture-bound way humans view species to understanding that the recognition of species is not just cultural, *it's fundamental to the argument that culture exists.*

Notes

1. Dipesh Chakrabarty, "The Climate of History: Four Theses," *Critical Inquiry* 35, no. 2 (2009): 197–222.

2. Ibid., 218.

3. Ibid.

4. Ibid., 213.

5. Ibid., 221.

6. Marx, "Economic and Philosophical Manuscripts," in *The Marx-Engels Reader,* ed. Robert Tucker (New York: W. W. Norton, 1978), 76.

7. Chakrabarty, "Climate of History," 220.

8. Michel Foucault, *The History of Sexuality, Volume One* (New York: Vintage Books, 1990), 142.

9. Ibid., 137.

10. Ibid., 142.

11.   Michel Foucault, *Security, Territory, Population* (New York: Picador, 2007), 67.

12.   Ibid., 67–68.

13.   Ibid., 75; emphasis added.

14.   Ibid.; emphasis added.

15.   Ibid., 78.

16.   Jody Hey, "On the Failure of Modern Species Concepts," *Trends in Ecology and Evolution* 21, no. 8 (2006): 254.

17.   Ibid., 259.

The Fables as Form

Aesop's Fables are cultural forms that circulate through a variety of mediums, surfacing or lying just out of sight in a host of contexts. Following Goankar and Povenelli, analyzing cultural forms requires that we not assume they're transparent, in the hopes of reading the social ideology "behind" the form, but attend instead to the social life of the form as it circulates.[1] Rather than serving as ciphers for the social, cultural forms, as they circulate, highlight the shifting interpretive conventions brought to bear in facilitating their movement, revealing "cultures of circulation." The questions to ask are not what they mean but why they travel and how they are rendered commensurate.[2] What forms of commensuration, then, can we see in the fables, especially in relation to species thinking? There are at least two. First, they stage other species as capable of speaking to us. This is, of course, not unfettered or human speech; the fables can rightfully all be charged with ventriloquizing nonhumans in shamelessly moralistic manners. But they do present both the possibility and problem of how we might listen to and then learn from other species.[3] As in species thinking, the predicaments of nonhumans are seen as having bearing on our situations and being entangled in our fate and livelihoods.[4] The fables are an argument that other species are worthy of attention for more than their functional uses, because we may be able or need to learn something from them.

Second, the fables frame the perils and potentials of species thinking. This mode of thought, we are reminded via Aesop's stockpile of tales, is never very far from the allegorical. For naturalism, this may be abhorrent, but for cultural anthropologists, this is rather a reminder of what we've long known about any forms of social analysis: they cannot be rendered without the inflections of myth and meaning, specifically for us, as humans. The fables are, in this sense, useful for recognizing what they misdiagnose or misunderstand through moralizing. But this dimension of both species thinking and the fables involves more than naturalizing—which an ideological analysis might conclude. Rather, the fables are concerned with and perform that most basic of cultural concerns: the transmissibility of experience, observation, and thought. In the fables, this is achieved by rendering select species as interlocutors in the midst of certain encounters—they wryly comment on each other's predicaments. In this sense, the fables are not so much—and certainly not uniquely so—about the naturalness of human characteristics as about glimpsing and imagining the sociality of other species.

Consider some of the scenes. One of the most frequently staged or imagined encounters is between species in domesticated spaces, mulling their relative positions and predicaments. A wild ass admiring a domesticated conspecific grazing fatly in a field (263),[5] switches to taunting when the tamed beast is harnessed to a heavy load. In "The Young Pig and the Sheep" (94), the pig is chastised for rude squealing when caught by the farmer; "we get caught by him constantly, and we don't make such a fuss." But the pig knows the difference between shearing and butchering. Similarly, a heifer gloating while watching an ox labor in the fields (92) is shocked to find herself religiously sacrificed, while the ox laughs and lives another day. Or the wood of a wagon axle complains to an ox: "we are the ones who carry all the burden and yet it is you who moan" (70). Trees speak often, sometimes of treachery by conspecifics who assault them in the form of ax handles (99) or wedges (100), and for delusions of grandeur for their role in shipbuilding, as mocked by a lowly bramble (101). A bat, similarly, ridicules a linnet (75) who now only sings at night, because singing in the day led to its capture—a lot of good such caution does now, the bat observes. This exchange, across the line of domestication, is one of many such commentary-provoking encounters: the olive tree taunts reeds over their modest stature, but they laugh last when the tree snaps in half during a storm (143). A jackdaw manages to "pass" amid "some well-fed pigeons in a pigeon-rearing aviary" by "whitening his plumage" (163). His ruse is revealed, after some time, when "he forgot himself and let out a cry." Cast out by the pigeons, the jackdaw is then rejected by his own, who no longer recognize him.

Pigeons are a staple character in such exchanges: used as snares, by a bird catcher, domesticated pigeons are chastised by captured wild ones—"being of the same race, they should have warned them of the trap." But the tamed version of the species relates that they're far too fearful of the master's displeasure to think that way (282). A pigeon, kept in a dovecote, boasted loudly of her fertility, until a crow wryly notes, "The more children you have, the more you should lament slavery" (302).

Playing a similar role as they did for Darwin, pigeons delineate the line between artificial and natural selection, so it is striking when one, driven by thirst (301), mistakes a painted water fountain for a real one and dies as a result. In contrast, when a partridge, caught and anticipating death, offers to cross the line into domestication by serving as a lure, the option is foreclosed by the hunter: "since you wish to ensnare your friends and comrades" (300). A similarly useful partridge protests its eventual butchering (285), reminding the bird catcher of its service as a lure: "All the more reason to sacrifice you, since you have not even had mercy on your own kindred." Along with bird catchers (and gardeners, fisherman, and plowmen), another major category of human laborer is that of the shepherd, who is often called on to distinguish species (5, 311–18), most famously the wolf trying to mimic a sheep. These occupations all involve multispecies relations, their management, and the forms of discernment they require. Such moments of recognition are accompanied by another set of scenes that have particular bearing on species thinking. These are moments of short-sightedness where a species's usefulness goes unacknowledged, generally with unfortunate results. A stork accidently snared by a bird catcher warns of her usefulness in eating "snakes and other reptiles," but the moralizing hunter condemns her "for landing among the wicked" cranes (284). Travelers disparage a "plane tree" (257) as "sterile and useless to man," neglecting to observe how they were benefiting from its shade. Within the circle of domestication, these also feature the perils of care—a beekeeper viciously stung by his enraged bees (235), mistaking him for a thief: "you mercilessly persecute me, who takes care of you." Care, notably, can be misplaced with other species (17, 313).

But the bigger problem is not recognizing the advantages bestowed by other life-forms. So learns the hind, hiding from hunters amid a thick stand of vines (103), where she feels free to eat the plentiful leaves, thereby revealing herself to the huntsmen: dying, she relates, "I ought not to have damaged that which could save me." A crab, straying from the protective sea to the exposed shore, is eaten by a fox (150) and similarly laments, "I deserve this fate." Meanwhile, among the domesticates, the billy goat is similarly schooled by a vine sporting young shoots, which he eats, even though green grass is nearby. The vine haughtily observes that it will still be around after providing wine to go along with the goat's sacrifice (339). Such fables read not so much as ur-moments of ecological consciousness but as reflections on encounters across species lines.

Donna Haraway, in theorizing companion species, spends a good deal of time considering how forms of etiquette and politeness can govern such encounters: "to hold in regard, to respond, to look back reciprocally, to notice, to pay attention, to have courteous regard for, to esteem: all of that is tied to polite greeting, to constituting the polis, where and when species meet."[6] What to make, then, of the frequent derision, mockery, and contempt conveyed in Aesop's Fables, such as "The Sow and the Dog Insulting One Another" (329), or that betrayal (by other species or conspecifics) is such a common theme? Sometimes it stems from the moments of short-sightedness listed earlier, an inability to recognize species predicaments. But the more telling reason probably lies in the concern over domestication—articulating, policing, and transgressing that line. This point matters in two regards: first, Haraway's notion of companion species takes little cognizance of this major fault line (see Anthropocene in "Domestication"), even though the dog—that most domesticated of species—is the centerpiece for her reflections. Second, this line is often imagined and perhaps *realized* in relation to human domains of collective conflict and struggle: class and race. Perhaps the social here, more than just culture per se, is distinct in involving the division of labor. Or maybe it's the old line about familiarity and contempt, as rendered in "The Camel Seen for the First Time":

> When they first set eyes on a camel men were afraid. Awed by its huge size, they ran away. But when, in time, they realized its gentleness, they plucked up enough courage to approach it. Then, gradually realizing that it had no temper, they went up to it and grew to hold it in such contempt that they put a bridle on it and gave it to their children to lead. (148)

Notes

1. Dilip Parameshwar Gaonkar and Elizabeth A. Povinelli, "Technologies of Public Forms: Circulation, Transfiguration, Recognition," *Public Culture* 15, no. 3 (2003): 385–98.

2. As Brian Larkin writes, "for cultural circulation to occur, especially across boundaries of difference, modes of equivalence and commensuration have to be identified that allow an element to move from one tradition to another without being identified as illicit." Larkin, "Making Equivalences Happen: Commensuration and the Architecture of Circulation," in *Images That Move*, ed. Patricia Spyer and Mary Margaret Steedly, 237–57 (Santa Fe, N.M.: SAR Press, 2014).

3. Kelly Oliver, *Animal Lessons: How They Teach Us to Be Human* (New York: Columbia University Press, 2009).

4. See Eben Kirksey, *Freedom in Entangled Worlds: West Papua and the Architecture of Global Power* (Durham, N.C.: Duke University Press, 2012).

5. All fables here are referenced via the numbering system in Robert Temple's *The Complete Fables* (New York: Penguin, 1997).

6. Haraway, *When Species Meet*, 19; see also 23–24, 41–42, 92, 222.

11

Model Organisms

Species that serve as fables of naturalism today are called *model organisms.* Their significance lies in the lessons that can be wrought from them regarding other species, even onto big-meaning questions about "life itself." These are not forms of fancy from myth or legend; these species dwell in lab spaces and field sites and appear on the rigorously vetted pages of scientific journals. Their stories may spread from such sites, out through the media, and are taken up in any number of popular and fanciful versions of "the way things are." But they start out as empirical artifacts, though this doesn't undermine their parabalistic qualities or aspects. The topics they concern—life and death, health and sickness, cleverness and values—are strikingly similar to Aesop's Fables.

A basic economy informs model organisms: there are far too many species for us to know sufficiently thoroughly; and of this excess, most also make inconvenient objects of research and learning. For efficiency's sake, researchers privilege a select few life-forms through which to organize and operate lab-based science: those that are convenient to store, breed, and standardize. The key point is that, like the fables, these species are selected for their representativeness, depicting life processes, gene expression, and interactions with the environment (see "Homology"). In this economy of examples, capacity for extrapolation is key. The knowledge they generate *must be transferable across species lines and applicable to other life-forms.*

What are the criteria for this select few? Historically, the premium has been placed on rapid breeding—the capacity to spawn generation after generation of fairly uniform organisms. Interest in this characteristic has only heightened with the frantic pace of funding cycles and expectations for more publications. In recent decades, though, the size of a species's genome came to matter, too—the smaller the better, because these are more easily cataloged, with each gene highly accountable. In LANGE-

BIO, where I do fieldwork, *Arabidopsis* is a featured species for both rea-sons—even though this grass has little directly to do with "biodiversity" in Mexico that the lab is charged with studying.

The representational dynamics here are quite complicated, partly because, to be representative in this manner, these life-forms require a good deal of standardization—a special form of domestication not geared for many traditional ends (labor, sustenance, transportation, etc.) but strictly for knowledge production. The variability of all life-forms must be sufficiently squelched in these species so they can achieve the status of laboratory instruments. As a result, model organisms end up a bit oblique to their varyingly explicit or implicit reference point: humans. In *Science without Laws: Model Systems, Cases, and Exemplary Narratives*,[1] Creager and her colleagues note that, through the process of standardization, "they are not models in the traditional sense—they are not smaller versions of humans, and they do not exactly replicate our experiences or disease.... That is, model systems do not directly represent humans as models *of* them. Rather, they serve as *exemplars or analogues* that are probed and manipulated in the search for generic (and genetic) relationships."[2] Their "utility in producing generalities relies on the routine use of analogies to other examples and entities."[3] This is about transspecies experiences and learning—just what concerned Aesop and his audiences.

Creager and her colleagues argue that "the model-system approach so pervasive in biology compares with the use of cases, exemplars, and related methods in others field."[4] This is, then, not just about sameness across life-forms but between and across domains of knowledge production for social as well as natural sciences. "Case-based reasoning relies on relations of similarity rather than on conventional reductionism and treats specificity as a resource, not a problem."[5] In this cultivation of examples, the nuances of a species—rather than frustrating basic ques-tions—multiply its capacity to speak, so to speak, to the conditions of other life-forms. They achieve the same trick as the species in Aesop's Fables: they have an "individual" quality—behavioral traits, say—that are construed as typical, common, and familiar. Model organisms and crea-tures in the fables share "the characteristics of specificity, typicality, mate-riality, and complexity."[6]

Exemplary laboratory organisms arise with the industrialization of sci-entific research: mass-produced, standardized materials became critical to science oriented toward responding to (or creating) market demands and the requirements of extractive enterprises. Untamed types, selected from the wild, might not represent their own species terribly well, their particular genomes not depicting the breadth of variation in wider populations. But once in the realm of science, they became subject to an enormous amount of description and diagramming, which allows them to stand as biological norms rather than exemplars of their own exemplary species. As a case index, the model organism becomes a reference point as well to the further generation of more organisms as well as to the comparisons and contrasts that are at the center of case-based reasoning, whether in biology or sociology. Here analogy comes to the fore. Creager and her colleagues note that "analogies play a crucial role in linking worms and humans, particularly at the level of homologies between genes. It is these analogies that have given nematode worms their purchase in medical research."[7] But, "although model organisms are standardized in order to facilitate highly controlled biological experiments, their inherent complexity means that these systems are never fully understood and can continue to generate surprising results. Indeed, as models, they are no simpler biologically than the humans they illuminate by analogy."[8]

The exemplary status of an organism can alter in its career—take fruit flies, that penultimate model species, *Drosophila melanogaster*. Prized for its capacity to reveal genetic commonalities with other species, the fruit fly, in a study of genes linked to aggression, produced a finding about sociality instead. Research led by David J. Anderson (California Institute of Technology), aiming to establish gender differences in relation to aggression, did seem to encounter a transspecies commonality: a gene found in mammals, as well, that is similarly linked to aggression. But the research also "demonstrated another human-fly connection, showing that jilted male flies will turn to drink," reported James Gorman in the *New York Times*,[9] adding "that it was interesting that the researcher found a connection between flies and mammals for a social behavior, even though they did not set out to look for it." After many qualifiers about the difficulties and perils of linking genes and behaviors, the article concludes with what might be the larger lesson: "But it is clear that humans and flies have more in common than it might appear." Quoting Anderson: "Studying aggression in fruit flies can actually teach us something about some of the molecules that control aggression."

Perhaps it's not surprising that the same edition of the *New York Times* reported on the relatively long-running tenure of Dr. Thomas R. Insel as director of the National Institute of Mental Health (NIMH). Insel's own brain science research—aimed toward reducing "complex social behavior like pair bonding to neural biology"—found his model organism in the prairie vole, principally because it's monogamous, forming long-term pair bonds after mating. Insel surprised many colleagues by shifting the focus of NIMH toward neuroscience and genetics, away from broad behavioral research, arguably shifting from "mental health" and "psychosocial" dynamics toward an exclusive focus on brain research. This shift was impelled, Benedict Carey reports,[10] by a conviction that "the previous generation of biological research in psychiatry has largely been a disappointment, both in advancing basic science and in improving lives." Pharmacology has yielded lots of interventions but "nothing about the causes of mental illness." Carey observes, "The same is true of most research using 'animal models,' in which scientists try to create psychiatric problems in animals and study them." Much like the fables, then, such lessons are cherished for their crystalline intuitions, but they falter or fade in relevance in relation to the complexity of social dynamics.

Notes

1. Angela N. H. Creager, Elizabeth Lunbeck, and M. Norton Wise, *Science without Laws: Model Systems, Cases, Exemplary Narratives* (Durham, N.C.: Duke University Press, 2007).

2. Ibid., 2.

3. Ibid.

4. Ibid., 4.

5. Ibid., 4–5.

6. Ibid., 16.

7. Ibid., 7.

8. Ibid.

9. James Gorman, "To Study Aggression, a Fight Club for Flies," *New York Times*, February 4, 2014.

10. Benedict Carey, "Blazing Trails in Brain Science," *New York Times*, February 3, 2014.

12

Species in the News

When and why do species make the news? Reporters cover all kinds of stories about humans, in political, economic, religious, social, or criminal frames and narratives; these are the subjects that have defined news since the genre's inception. But it is increasingly easy to find reporting on nonhumans. How do these subjects become the focus of news coverage, and what are they able to convey about the predicaments of certain species? Much like the fables, the depicted nonhumans are posed in a manner to tell us something notable about the world, even though they follow the dictates of journalistic objectivity. And much like the fables, many of these stories are concerned with what a species may be able to communicate to us—what can they tell us, for instance, of the imminence of our own doom owing to climate change? But in the range of nonhumans making it into the news today, there's clearly more at work.

Most commonly, the species showing up in journalistic coverage are like the twenty-thousand-year-old handprints in caves in Spain and France: they depict an outline of the human in relief, cast via the uses we make of them or the investments they represent. Bees, for instance, are the subject of a great deal of reporting, because of the central role they play in agriculture. The mystery and uncertainty over the causes of colony collapse disorder feature compelling potential villains and heroes—pesticide manufacturers, nervous or financially strapped farmers, and various researchers trying to determine which of many possible causes or factors is the true "culprit." This is arguably, though, just a dramatic rendition of a basic story line concerning *commodity species*—plants or animals whose movement from field to processing plant to market and the dinner table is noteworthy because of their role in generating profits. From crops (coffee, corn) to producers (cranking out milk, eggs, meat, etc.), an array of species may be subject to coverage in routine reporting on price fluctuations, or they may shift into heightened focus when their availability is subject to change.

Such pursuits can, in turn, generate another significant genre of reporting on nonhumans. Though "at risk," bees have yet to slide over into the other common story subject, that of endangered species. These animals or plants and the accounts provided of them are also effective ledgers of human activity and interests, in a negative sense. Typically, these are species imperiled by the expansion of cities or the loss of habitat owing to extractive industries. Which "endangered species" are delaying projects or the subject of investment and concern? Occasionally, these organisms are not placed directly at risk by humans. Trees are dying across the United States because of both drought and expanding ranges of various insects that feed on their bark. This becomes a story because of the subsequent risks posed to humans, from heightened danger of fires, for instance, or because of the less measurable impact of loss of *scenic species*.

Such stories are generated largely because someone or some institution cares about the species in question. Coverage is conjured up by concerned citizens or scientists involved in conservation efforts. These stories may generate or be directed toward a public for whom the species could or should matter.[1] Ivory tusks and rhino horns ground stories for the U.S. audience of the terrible things done by foreigners to exotic species, some of which end up in zoos and preserves. This centuries-old practice has led to a new genre of stories featuring *species calculations*, when management takes over from care. The trope here is of "picking and choosing what makes it onto the ark," as David Greene commented at the opening of an NPR *Morning Edition* story about how efforts to save trumpeter swans in Montana have endangered a rare species of trout.[2] Similarly, Leslie Kaufman, in an article in the *New York Times*,[3] conveys how "zoos are increasingly being called upon to rescue and sustain animals" facing extinction—"not just for marquee breeds like Pandas and rhinos but also for all manner of mammals, frogs, birds, and insects." Of the "cold calculations" about which animals to save, she writes, "The burden feels less like Noah building an ark and more like Schindler making a list."

In these calculations and the ways publics respond to them, it is interesting to see the sociality of certain species develop some prominence. The Copenhagen Zoo stirred great outrage from their killing (by shotgun) of Marius, a healthy two-year-old giraffe. "Administrators said they had decided to kill Marius," Nelson Schwartz reported, "because his genes were well represented among captive giraffe populations in Europe."[4] To let him live and breed "would have opened the door to inbreeding and potentially removed a place for a giraffe whose genetic makeup was more valuable in terms of future offspring in captive breeding populations." This eugenic argument aside, why couldn't he be allowed live and be adopted by any number of individuals who offered to take him? Well, first off, as Bengt Holst, the zoo's scientific director, explained, "a giraffe is not a pet; it's not like a dog or cat that becomes part of the family. It's a wild animal." But just as crucially, "he said giraffes are social animals and could not be kept in isolation." Sociality is increasingly seen, also, as a basis for "saving" animals from captivity in zoos or animal parks. The *Blackfish* video on CNN[5] (and *The Cove* documentary[6] as well) makes the case that the species most like us—intelligent, with complex social organizations—should not be kept captive. This argument has gradually expanded, shifting as a public discourse, from arguments against inhumane treatment of animals who could individually suffer to assertions that those most approximating us socially—with strong family bonds and sophisticated communicative capacity—should not be caged.

Speaking of, "like us," another genre of species stories, involving microbes, is leading to an incipient revision of what it means to be human. Interestingly, this genre inverts or perhaps runs in parallel with a strand of journalism on species that directly threaten us, via illness and disease. The new bent in this category is a surge of stories about bacteria and microbes that are actually beneficial, and perhaps even essential, to human existence. "Bacteria in the Intestine May Help Tip the Bathroom Scale, Studies Show," read a headline in the *New York Times,*[7] reporting on research on how gut microbes might play a role in weight gain or loss. This subject, in particular, shows how attending to certain species can lead to a "ground"-up reenvisioning of the human, as in Michael Pollan's "Some of My Best Friends Are Germs."[8] Stories about microbes are also a basis for shifting conceptions of gardening (see "What Is a Garden?") from something you do outdoors to plants to something that we do inside our body with organisms we'll never see.

The important question to pose is this: *when does the intuition start buzzing that this is about "us" as a species?* In a cursory and initial gesture, responses might be typed as follows: (1) when it confirms a cultural discourse; (2) when it challenges one; (3) when it's an opportunity to think in a different way about collective forms of identity. This latter category opens up now to include species that share with us the capacity to transform environments. Another story in the *New York Times*[9] reported on the work of Norbert Juergens (University of Hamburg) on a species of sand termites, *Psammotermes allocerus,* who occupy a desert belt from Angola to

Namibia. The reporter, John Noble Wilford, characterized the termites' activities "as examples of natural ecosystem engineering by a particular species," who can be seen as "agents for making much of their desert home an oasis of permanent grassland. It's not hard to see a glimmer of curiosity here informed by the precarity of humans' desert dwellings in the United States as drought takes a greater toll on the West. Hence, perhaps we could learn something from a species that "turns wide desert regions of predominantly ephemeral life into landscapes dominated by species-rich perennial grasslands supporting uninterrupted perennial life even during dry seasons and drought years." These termites previously fell under the purview of anthropologists who recorded folk stories from the Himba people about these grassy rings as "footprints of the gods," made by the "original ancestors." Wilford reports that "a just-so story blames a mythical dragon that lives beneath the earth. The dragon's poisonous breath kills vegetation to create the circles." Here the termite circles moved from fable into the domain of science research largely through aerial and satellite photo analysis, thus correcting native lore and expanding the domain of science.[10] But the larger significance may be in glimpsing species that might be having parallel effects on the environment, or species whose capacity to do so intrigues us.

But there may be more diffuse forms of attention developing toward nonhumans yet to come. In the wake of Typhoon Haiyan in the Philippines, the *New York Times* ran an unusual image on the front page, above the fold: an overhead shot of trees leveled by the storm. There are no people in the scene, no cluttered city streets or collapsed buildings; it's an image notable for its lack of humans and largely devoid of their built forms. The photo—captioned "Uprooted coconut trees near Guiuan in the Philippines, which was devastated by Typhoon Haiyan's winds and storm surge"—is also unusual because these trees don't fit the common frame for reporting on nonhuman species: they are not endangered, nor were they particularly picturesque. Presumably, they're cultivars, and this is an orchard of some sort. But the story gives no further details than provided in the caption. It's just an odd acknowledgment of the "natural" toll of a "natural disaster" on domesticated species.

Notes

1. Hartigan, "Plant Publics," *Anthropological Quarterly*, forthcoming.

2. David Greene, NPR *Morning Edition*, July 18, 2013.

3. Leslie Kaufman, "Zoo's Bitter Choice," *New York Times*, May 27, 2012.

4. Nelson Schwartz, "Anger Erupts after Danish Zoo Kills a 'Surplus' Giraffe," *New York Times*, February 10, 2014.

5. http://www.cnn.com/SPECIALS/us/cnn-films-blackfish.

6. http://www.imdb.com/title/tt1313104/.

7. *New York Times*, March 28, 2013.

8. *New York Times*, May 15, 2013.

9. John Noble Wilford, "Fairy Circles in Africa May Be Work of Termites," *New York Times*, March 29, 2013.

10. The origin of these artifacts remains subject to debate, and the role of termites is being questioned by recent research that suggests that the circles are the product of self-regulating grass growth. See Stephan Getzin, Kerstin Wiegand, Thorsten Wiegand, Hezi Yizhaq, Jost von Hardenberg, and Ehud Meronm, "Adopting a Spatially Explicit Perspective to Study the Mysterious Fairy Circles of Namibia," *Ecography* 37 (2014): 1–11.

13

Identifying Species

The philosophical and metaphysical conundrums presented by the concept of species are immense. That a simple fault line traverses this immensity—between biological or genetic definitions—belies the expanse of theoretical and methodological controversies and issues entailed by identifying species, either classifying "new" ones or locating existing ones amid mutable taxonomical criteria and schemas. Much of this complexity seems to dissipate in the face of developing technologies that heighten our capacities to identify and observe species, though maybe without knowing them any better than we do now—just recognizing them more efficiently. New techniques, such as DNA bar coding, satellite and cellular tagging, and drones, help alleviate much of our inability to recognize species, making them more familiar and accessible, but without contributing much yet to the taxonomic knowledge projects concerned with species. That is, these developing abilities to monitor and track species open a critical rift with the centuries-old endeavors to know species through classification.

DNA bar coding is increasingly in the news, though its role in taxonomy and biology is somewhat disparaged. This technology is about identifying rather than discovering and classifying species; its uses are principally aimed toward regulatory and commercial concerns and functions, more than epistemological projects. The overarching goal toward which it is directed is moving species steadily toward ever-growing catalogs—that cultural form whose meanings and uses remain principally defined by the marketing innovation by Montgomery Ward in 1872, as the primary mechanism behind his mail-order empire. Not surprisingly, the technology's inventor, Paul D. N. Herbert (University of Guelph), conceived of it as he reflected on the singular capacity of a single form—the barcode—to identify, track, and properly shelve all of the items in a supermarket.[1] Today its uses are largely regulatory and commercial; it represents an effort at standardizing species, or our recognition of them, reflecting a principal concern with markets rather than taxonomy; this is principally applied to species that already have established niches in our commodity chains.

The growing applications of this technology reflect a fundamental unfamiliarity with the species, or at least their commodity forms, of which we are most fond. This was revealed in the news item that brought DNA bar coding into public awareness. In 2011, the *Boston Globe* published the results of a major investigative report on the mislabeling of fish in area restaurants—their core finding: 48 percent of the fish sold to consumers was billed with the wrong species name.[2] Undesirable species—hake, escolar, or haddock, for instance—replaced popular, prized, and presumably more flavorful ones, such as cod, red snapper, and white tuna. Strikingly, no customers seemed to have noticed; chefs and producers often pleaded ignorance, too, based on a widespread inability to recognize the difference between species once the fish was filleted. For that matter, a follow-up investigation one year later netted much the same results, with little or no change in mislabeling practices, suggesting that consumers had not grown more discerning about the species they were eating.[3]

But the testing technology certainly took off. The basic technique, developed in 2003 by Hebert, is intriguing because its foundation lies in keying on crosscutting sameness for all species: a few commonly shared genes—*CO1* for animals; two chloroplast genes (*rbcL* and *matK*) in plants; and the internal transcribed spacer (ITS) region with fungi. Any sampled specimen can yield a DNA sequence that "can be used to identify different species, in the same way a supermarket scanner uses the familiar black stripes of the UPC barcode to identify your purchases," according to the International Barcode of Life. The Boston reporters, over a five-month period, sent samples for testing to the Biodiversity Institute, University of Guelph, where Herbert is based. Specimens' DNA was extracted and read for a gene fragment that was then matched with items in the institute's library, the Barcode of Life Data System, or BOLD. Reporters similarly explained to their readers that this technique is called bar coding, "because, just as a supermarket scanner reads a barcode to distinguish beans from milk, the DNA snippet separates one species from another." Directly following this report, the U.S. Food and Drug Administration (FDA), which maintains a list of acceptable market names for species, went public with its own DNA database for bar coding frequently consumed species. Their collection features specimens identified by taxonomists at the Smithsonian Institution. The FDA, though it had been working with scientists at the University of Guelph, opted to build its own library because the one in Guelph was "not designed to be a regulatory database."[4]

More than fraud is associated with misidentifying species. The report revealed the perils and complications of the massive commodity chains that bring fish to American tables. With imported seafood comprising close to 90 percent of the fish Americans eat, problems arise from where the fish were caught to how they were processed and marketed. The problems with mislabeling fish range from putting diners at risk of allergic reactions or exposure to chemicals banned in the United States to undermining conservation efforts. "Seafood substitution makes it harder for consumers to accept that some species, including red snapper, are overfished, since it regularly appears on restaurant menus." As well, there is the profiteering of marketing "high-value species," then switching them out on the plate for less expensive ones.

DNA bar coding highlights the variety of ways we bunch and characterize species—"disease vector species," "invasive" and "conservation" species, as well as "provisional" or "vouchered" species and "cryptic species complexes." The first set of these labels reflects distinct interests and concerns as varied as public health or landscaping or climate change; the second stems from the knowledge apparatus by which we scientifically classify species. DNA bar coding is drifting somewhere between these distinct orientations—interested versus ostensibly neutral or at least objective. The bar coding approach is not designed for classification; rather, it relies entirely on orienting samples to specimens that have been authoritatively connected to a species name by a taxonomist and stored somewhere.

Bar coding detaches and dissolves species being—its relationship to a genus, an environment, and a phylogeny—by distilling and rendering it as a genetic sequence that can be uniquely associated with one previously established taxon. This is not as abstract as it might sound and involves concrete sites and objects. The dematerializing of species identification can only go so far, at the moment. The database or library is of little or no value without being linked to a collection of physical specimens. Vouchered species are grounded by specimens stored in natural history collections and herbariums. Yet out beyond the familiar commodified and entertaining species—many of which we evidently face some difficulty in naming—stretches the great, vast expanse of unknown species. In this domain of "biodiversity," bar coding is, as of yet, minimally useful.

Bar coding obscures something very important about taxonomy: taxa are hypotheses. They are inherently contingent formulations waiting to be possibly revaluated and disproved. In such cases, specimens may move from one species to another, fracture into multiple species, or shift genera. The risk with the bar code form and "library" database is that it can become detached from these specimens, while taxonomic concepts, theories, and classifications change. This ever tentative aspect of taxonomic knowledge involves ongoing revisions of species descriptions and phylogenies. Social theorists often construe taxonomy as a project of emphatic, absolute domination of life-forms, tyrannically steering them all into tiny boxes. But taxonomists are continually open both to new data and new visions, sharing in a recognition that deep time, with its barely perceptible shifts and transformations or hybridization of species, could prove their formulations wrong.

Puillandre and colleagues frame the problem thus: "When DNA sequences are used as a tag to identify specimens, how can the link be maintained in the long term between the DNA barcodes (which provide the name to the user) and the expert-identified specimens?"[5] The problem that played out on the plates of diners who were provided one name and served a different specimen is linked to a bigger epistemological problem. With the rise of molecular analysis of species in the 1990s, "the tight link between the collection, the name, the species concepts and the scientist's work was loosened, and some of us forgot that behind the sequences were real objects: the specimens, which are representative of populations of living organisms."[6] Taxonomists remain leery of bar coding, knowing how easily these links are undone, so applications and innovations of this technology are increasingly oriented to consumers. Herbert now envisions—and hopes to develop and market—handheld devices deployed in dining rooms or supermarkets, as much as in jungles or biopreserves.

The Barcode of Life imagines its role as "Building a Bioliterate World"; its website homepage asks, "What would it be like to live in a bio-literate world—a world where you could know, in minutes, the name of any animal or plant—anytime, anywhere? And not just its name but everything about it—what are its habits, is it endangered, is it dangerous, should it even be there or is it an invader from somewhere else?"[7] This knowledge will likely require handheld devices that can be marketed as conveyors of forms of identification detached from the processes of knowledgably identifying species. It's a knowledge that a potentially dwindling number of taxonomists now carry around in their heads.

Notes

1. Nicholas Wade, "A Species in a Second: Promise of DNA 'Bar Codes,'" *New York Times*, December 4, 2004.

2. Jenn Abelson and Beth Daley, "On the Menu, but Not on Your Plate," *Boston Globe*, October 23, 2011, http://www.boston.com/business/articles/2011/10/23/on_the_menu_but_not_on_your_plate/?p1=News_links.

3. Jenn Abelson and Beth Daley, "New Round of DNA Tests Finds Dozens of Repeat Offenders in Fish Mislabeling," *Boston Globe*, October 1, 2012.

4. Clare Leschin-Hoar, "Specious Species: Fight against Seafood Fraud Enlists DNA Testing," *Scientific American*, November 10, 2011.

5. N. Puillandre, P. Bouchet, M.-C. Boisselier-Dubayle, J. Brisset, B. Buge, M. Castelin, S. Chagnoux et al., "New Taxonomy and Old Collections: Integrating DNA Barcoding into the Collection Curation Process," *Molecular Ecology Resources* 12, no. 3 (2012): 396–402.

6. Ibid.

7. http://ibol.org/.

14

Domestication

It is hard to get "beyond the human" when we reside in the Anthropocene—that geological age characterized by the massive transformative (and perhaps imperiling) effect humans have had on the planet. An urge impelling much multispecies work is to somehow transcend or at least badly rupture anthropocentrism. This might not be best accomplished via the model of going "beyond" but rather by considering the muddled terrain "between" the human and nonhuman, that of domestication. Here a breach in human-centered thinking is opening in ongoing efforts at reconsidering this process by which culture bends and shapes biology.[1] This subject matters because here anthropocentrism confronts anthropomorphism—human-centered perspectives contend with human-shaped life-forms and concepts. The core certainty and conceit behind a long tradition of narrating the history of domestication is that, simply, it's *something we did to them.* Humans domesticated other species, plants, and animals. The rupture that opens in anthropocentrism today exactly arises from the recognition and/or speculation that we may not have been the principal agents of domestication: *they might have done it to us* or at least played an active role in the production of companion specieshood that has so transformed the globe.

Instead of a narrative that depicts it as singular, human-guided achievement in dominating and exploiting plant and animal species, a more fitful and uncertain account of domestication is emerging from anthropology. We see a concerted effort to "replace the unidirectional, progressive history of increasingly exploitative relationships with the environment with a more halting and incomplete vision, in which the experience of sheep and goats, for example, are [*sic*] placed against more ambiguous stories of microbes and weeds. In this competing vision, emphasis has been placed on mutual interaction between humans and nonhuman species, and the variety of cultural strategies that are employed in managing human and nonhuman resources, the role of animals and the environment in this negotiation, and the changing balance between exploitation, accommodation, and mutuality."[2] Out of this reconsideration arises an opportunity to rethink not just our assumptions about arrows and agents but the fundamental delineation of biology and sociology.

This new perspective has particular bearing on social theory and its principal conviction that our understanding of the world is entirely framed through projections informed by (and that read back to us) the organization of social life. In reconsidering domestication, though, we see first that sociality (nonhuman and human versions) likely served as the transpecies medium by which domestication could be effected; second, the evident dynamisms of species as life-forms suggests social theory has underestimated or misconstrued how thought travels across species lines. Rather than promoting inherently typological or essentialist modes of thought, instances of domestication suggest the "natural" order is far from static and is eminently pliable, that is, not a firm ideological basis or "ground" on which to sanction and replicate a particular social hierarchy. "Nature" is rather equivocal on the matter of fixity, after all.

Domestication is a good reminder that the life-forms Darwin relied on first to glimpse and then to articulate the theory of evolution were ones subject to "artificial selection." Pigeons, dogs, cabbages, and horses—all identified as "races" by Darwin—were the means by which he came to posit a process of "natural selection." Such projections should not be read as merely affirming the social theorists' stance that we can never escape cultural representations. Because what is at stake here is a range of life-forms that illustrate the capacity of culture to operate on the biological—arguably, a far more important and useful stance than maintaining anything worth talking about is reducible to a "social construction." The creatures Darwin turned to, much as did Aesop some twenty-five hundred years prior, are the ones that make clear that culture is not isolable to one side or the other in delineations of human and nonhuman. More importantly, culture is not simply "in our heads" as a collective representation but rather is at work transforming the world all around us. Isn't that the central realization of the Anthropocene?

Characterizations of the Anthropocene arise not just from the recognition that 80 percent of the planet's land surface has been modified by humans but also that humans and our domesticated species compose some 90 percent of today's vertebrate biomass. The last ten thousand years or so of domestication have featured a massive expansion of human culture over nonhuman life-forms. But did common forms of culture or equivalent capacities for sociality play a role in this extension? This is all about arrows and agents—which direction do causal arrows point, and who are the agents directing them? Certainty about directionality hardly needs to be established before granting that *this is the fundamental ground in which the human and nonhuman are inextricable*—not just as "messmates"[3] bound together in ecological entanglements of evolution that may be millions of years old (natural selection) but as life-forms drawn together in historical time in transformative acts that form the basis for modern society, "artificial selection."

What's at stake here is something akin to a figure or ground shift, but one where subject and object reverse fields. Journalist Michael Pollan, in *Botany of Desire*, conveys this perspectival shift as he experienced it himself, one day in the garden, watching bees busily attending to the blossoms and pollen of an apple tree—an activity that mirrored his own efforts sowing rows below its branches. "All these plants, which I'd always regarded as the objects of my desire, were also, I realized, subjects, acting on me, getting me to do things for them they couldn't do for themselves."[4] He cited "a failure of imagination"—on his part and that of the bees—as stunting this intuition: "The truth of the matter is that the flower has cleverly manipulated the bee into hauling its pollen from blossom to blossom"; "consciousness needn't enter into it on either side, and the traditional distinction between subject and object is meaningless." This insight launched his effort to "take seriously the plant's point of view" concerning four domesticated species—apples, tulips, marijuana, and potatoes—that "have spent the last ten thousand or so years figuring out how best to feed, heal, clothe, intoxicate, and otherwise delight us,"[5] that we propagate them more widely and fully.

A more fully social account of this intuition is developed by geographer Paul Robbins, in *Lawn People: How Grasses, Weeds, and Chemicals Make Us Who We Are*. Regarding "the lawn as a political and economic network,"[6] Robbins asks, who hails the homeowner or renter to attend to its expansive need? Consider: this activity often entails people acting against their self-interests, incurring huge expense while putting neighborhood children (and the environment) at risk to various chemical exposures—homeowners use up to ten times more chemicals per acre than do farmers. Initially, he felt that "the explanation seems compelling for social structures"[7]—civic codes and their enforcers, neighbors and their castigating looks. "Yet it really says very little about the daily interactions that actually dominate people's lives and human behaviors in nature, economy, and community. In the case of vast ecologies, what does the interpellating?" He answers succinctly, "It may be the lawn itself. Desire and diazinon are demanded by lawns, if not by the grasses that constitute them." That's because the humans are so attuned to the grass, "its signals are apparent to homeowners, whose response is an act of subjection, not only to the lawn, but also to the ideology of community and the international economy of turf maintenance."[8]

In this analysis, the lawn as "an object, helps to construct the subject," or "Turfgrass Subjects"[9] more specifically. But this extended (to nonhuman) social analysis also opens directly onto the Anthropocene and Chakrabarty's "deep history." Robbins acknowledges that "the evolutionary history of grasses, especially turfgrasses, is notably intertwined with that of humanity. Many of the earth's grasses have coevolved with domesticated livestock and their wild ancestors over the last 100,000 years. . . . Our relationship with grasses is therefore prehistorically deep and turfgrass cover has been with human civilization for a very long time, in some form or another." Most importantly, "of the fifteen major world crops today, ten of them are grasses (including wheat, maize, millet, and rice)."[10] This analysis is notable both for its perspective on grass and also for how it comes to terms with—by way of incorporating or relying on—the very subjects social theorists have sought to foreclose an attention to: evolution and biological theories and narratives.

Social theorists consistently eschew and castigate evolutionary narratives involving people because of their ideological impacts in (1) rationalizing and reproducing social hierarchies and (2) blunting the very deployment and development of a social analysis of cultural dynamics and phenomena. Indeed, Robbins is at pains to dismiss invocations of a mystical or genetic "nostalgia" for and connection to "our savanna-dwelling Australopithecine ancestors."[11] Rather, in his account, this evolutionary framework effectively indicts these turfgrass subjects as participating in the same ecological imperialism (citing Crosby) that devastated both indigenous peoples and grasses—a process of interrelated extermination attempts that paralleled the "mutually produced" contemporary American society and environment, which "evolve[ed] as a team."[12] It also destabilizes the neat delineation Darwin maintained between "artificial" and "natural" selections.

The problem that social theorists might have with this confluence of thoughts and analytical registers may not involve the ways they blur or combine biology and sociality, but too many accounts of domestication don't yet do this effectively. As Rebecca Cassidy and Molly Mullin relate, "definitions of domestication generally stress either the biological or the social aspects."[13] The biological frame focuses on how controls on breeding, feeding, and movement result in biological changes. The social focuses on the transformation of animals into property as the key to domestication, which in turn produced changes in human interactions along with those between people and nonhumans. But like kinship, domestication is "inherently simultaneously biological and social."[14] Domestication, exactly because it entangles humans and nonhumans so thoroughly, also confounds biology and society as distinct registers—as does the Anthropocene, as a concept, though including geology and the environment as well. This all should be of particular relevance to social theorists who are concerned not just with the ideological uses of nature to ratify social hierarchy but also with operations of dehumanization, as with race, where the line around humanity is delimited such that categories of conspecifics are cast out into the domains of the nonhuman—often on the basis of imagined and asserted resemblance to dogs, pigs, and apes. Domestication gets us not only into "deep time"—complicating convenient narratives about the "idea of race" as a modern invention—but also into the biological, a domain that still makes many social theorists queasy. Both of these domains upset the primacy of the social, especially in terms of the directional arrow by which, "since Durkheim," society has been ideologically projected onto nature as a means of affirming and reproducing hierarchies. The tangle of directional arrows or agency suggested by a more fulsome account of domestication will be nettlesome to analysts who are convinced that all this traffic largely runs one way.

Notes

1. Rebecca Cassidy and Molly Mullin, *Where the Wild Things Are Now: Domestication Reconsidered* (New York: Berg, 2004).

2. Ibid., 6.

3. Haraway, *When Species Meet.*

4. Michael Pollan, *Botany of Desire* (New York: Random House, 2001), xv.

5. Ibid., xvi.

6. Paul Robbins, *Lawn People: How Grasses, Weeds, and Chemicals Make Us Who We Are* (Philadelphia: Temple University Press, 2007), 14.

7. Ibid., 16.

8. Ibid.

9.   Ibid.

10.   Ibid., 18–19.

11.   Ibid., 19.

12.   Ibid., 21–24.

13.   Cassidy and Mullin, *Where the Wild Things Are Now*, 30.

14.   Ibid., 38.

15

Have Culture, Will Travel

Most researchers agree that the concept of culture should be applied to animals and humans alike, in order to stress its continuity from one to the other and not withstanding the immensely greater complexity of human behavior.
—*E. O. Wilson*

Wilson's summary assessment here may not surprise many biologists, but I think it might be news to social theorists. When did that modality we so long reserved as distinct from biology—the very basis for asserting things like that science and biology are socially constructed—slip away from us? Obviously, this occurred over the last couple decades, when the culture concept was viewed with suspicion and outright hostility by many cultural anthropologists, a period that coincided with the term's rapid spread onto newspaper business pages ("corporate culture"), into medical practice ("cultural competency"), and into many other popular domains ("culture of corruption"). In this broader usage, "culture," curiously, now vies against the increasingly popular gesture of invoking DNA—as in a company's orientation ("it's in our DNA")—to characterize things like ethos and *geist*.

For social theorists who may be squeamish about this realization, it's worth noting that an outgrowth of thinking about culture across species lines is the recognition of its fundamental capacity to shape genes. Not quickly or facilely, but over long stretches of time, culture works on the genes of humans and nonhumans alike. How culture achieves this, and how it does so similarly in a variety of species, is a provocative question. Yet another option for breaching the "golden barrier" that conceptually regards the human version of culture as unique and removed from all other species is via evolution. We only have culture because that capacity was passed on to us evolutionarily. Both of these points are touchstones for E. O. Wilson's discussion of culture in *The Social Conquest of*

Earth, which addresses "the questions of where we came from and what we are" through a survey of recent research on the origins and propagation of "advanced social life."[1] If you're familiar at all with Wilson, it will come as no surprise that his inquiry is formulated by juxtaposing culture in relation to humans and certain insects, by "putting insects next to people." The lessons learned here are oriented toward an array of schoolings gleaned from other species about us. But they also should remind us of the historical, genocidal problems with more specific versions of this alignment.[2]

> Biologists have turned with great success to the bacteria and yeast to learn the principles of human molecular genetics. They have depended on roundworms and mollusks to learn the basis of our neural organization and memory. And fruit flies have taught us a great deal about the development of human embryos. We have no less to learn from the social insects, in this case to add background to the origin and meaning of humanity.[3]

From this tradition of research lessons, Wilson adds or highlights the action of culture on genes—and, of course, vice versa. "Gene-culture coevolution, the impact of genes on culture and, reciprocally, culture on genes, is a process of equal importance to the natural sciences, the social sciences, and the humanities. Its study provides a way to connect these three great branches with a network of causal explanations."[4] The notion of causality may be disturbing to social theorists whose preference for "overdetermination" and "complexity" makes causality seem reductive and deterministic. But that culture shapes genes (and thus the human genome[5]) is critically important, certainly for contesting the geneticization of race but also for exactly challenging deterministic accounts of social condition linked to biology. And Wilson is far from being reductive: "The intricacies of gene-culture coevolution are fundamental to understanding the human condition. They are complex and at first may seem strange, being unfamiliar."[6] Moreover, Wilson envisions a division of labor that social theorists could probably work with: "How to think out and deal with the eternal ferment generated by multilevel selection is the role of the social sciences and humanities," because "the social sciences and humanities are devoted to the proximate, outwardly expressed phenomena of human sensations and thought."[7] He even sounds quite a bit like Geertz in praising "the infinite stories that human relationships can generate."[8]

The terrain Wilson invites us to traverse, in following the extent of sociality across the evolutionary spectrum, is not one that features singular, simplistic causal operators. The key point is plasticity, a matter already at the core of culture. This is, perhaps, what biologists gain in this discussion of transspecies modes of sociality. The question social theorists might pose here is what bearing, if any at all, these developmental and origin narratives may have on the contemporary dynamics that interest cultural anthropologists today—what we refer to as power–history. Or, more pointedly, do these lessons that claim to convey the *origins* of culture tell us anything about *sociality in the current moment*?

Decidedly, the viewpoint of Wilson and others who think about culture crossing species lines is oriented "backward," into deep evolutionary time. In such a view, the wreckage glimpsed by Walter Benjamin's Angel of History is inconsequential or scarcely yet apparent. "History" pertains to the geological "second" of time we occupy, which, in turn, is dwarfed by the scope and scale of evolution. But the take-away, as it were, from this perspective is that "we did not invent culture. The common ancestor of chimpanzees and prehumans invented it."[9] It only makes sense, then, that *we encounter culture when we look across species boundaries*: our version came from theirs. Deep history aside, a considerably more important point is that common cultural mechanisms operate out of this shared evolutionary commons—in particular, imitation, an activity of increasing interest for social theorists, for which many have returned to Tarde's writings (see "The Social (re)Turn"). In highlighting imitation as a transspecies aspect of culture, Wilson is obliged to offer an important reminder: the "property of cultural variation is the likelihood the individual group members imitate others in the same society have adapted the trait ('sensitivity to usage pattern')."[10] The important question is, what does culture let us see about species, our own and others? Fundamentally, it highlights their plasticity, morphologically as well as behaviorally—exactly what culture highlights in relation to humans.

The core of Wilson's discussion of culture–gene interactions is plasticity. This may surprise social theorists who are expecting typological or essentialist thinking. No, if anything, evolution shows that species are dynamic, not static or fixed. But this dynamism really expands when culture enters the picture. "The expression of genes may be plastic, allowing a society to choose one or more traits from a multiplicity of choices."[11] This view builds "up" from the "familiar example of varying plasticity in anatomical traits," which Wilson finds "easily applied as well to cultural traits."[12] It's not long before all the anxieties and angers generated by sociobiology surface again, even though he allows that culture shapes genes. His view is reminiscent of eugenics and its utter contemporaneousness: "All societies and each of the individuals in them play games of genetic fitness, the rules of which have been shaped across countless generations by gene-culture coevoultions."[13] The connection of "rules," "fitness," and "genes" may make the social theorist squeamish, as would Wilson's extended example of this form of genetic–cultural plasticity. But if such views are not able to be expulsed—and no amount of social constructionist argument has achieved this yet—then it's far better to engage them and work studiously at refiguring them, exactly through the frame of culture linking humans and nonhumans.

In this view, it matters that Wilson's account reviews the reasons why his earlier concept of sociobiology was subject to such scathing critique by cultural anthropologists. More than just an account of the world "as it is," he also reminds us of the social critique that such accounts are always ideologically informed and interested. It is not the case that we should ever jettison that critical social perspective. But can the old stories be turned to open up new ways of thinking? Alongside countless renditions of the-ant-as-fable, Wilson writes, "Ants and other social insects illustrate to an extreme degree the evolution of adaptive plasticity,"[14] as is common, turning immediately to the division of labor. "The workers of ant or termite colonies often differ so much from one another that they can easily be mistaken as belonging to separate species"—as, he might add, humans have been wont to do with cultural perceptions of racial difference. Not surprisingly, "caste" enters in here. "Yet, in colonies with a single queen who mated with only one male, all the castes of a gender are close to being genetically identical."[15]

This observation has new meaning given recent works on epigenetics and bears importantly on the biological basis for the disturbing differences of life expectancy by race in the United States (that whites live five years longer, on average, than blacks). It's not genetics that produces or explains such stunning differences. "They are distinct in anatomy and behavior because as immature forms they were given either more food or less than others, leading to larger or smaller adults." Tissues, subsequently, grow at different rates, generating "different body proportions," and pheromones play a role as well, "altering the directions of development and how large they grew before reaching maturity."[16] This opens onto epigenetics, a dynamic of central importance to understanding racial disparities and their causes today. What's interesting is the connection that follows, between "epigenetic rules and the propensity to imitate others, both of which have originated by gene-culture coevolution."[17] As Tarde suggested, society can be defined by the capacity and willingness of organisms to imitate each other, even to the extent of remolding our physiologies in conformance with social hierarchies.

But there's another option or potential direction in Wilson's lesson about ants and people, one that lurks in the foreground of "deep history" associated with plasticity: cultivation. Evolutionary time is not as relevant here, largely because the processes of most import developed in the last ten thousand years or so, when "modern humans" were already evolved into our "us" today. What does matter in this more recent segment of deep history is domestication, the activity that gives us the Anthropocene. And here a different cadre of species comes to the fore: not those who are socially "advanced," like us, but those with whom our achievement of cultivation became possible. And with its advent, we have culture in a rather different mode, a modality that fundamentally required engagements and encounters across species lines, where culture is already active and influential.

Notes

1. Wilson, *Social Conquest of Earth*, 10.
2. Hugh Raffles, *Insectopedia* (New York: Pantheon, 2010).
3. Wilson, *Social Conquest of Earth*, 10.
4. Ibid., 236.
5. Laland et al., "How Culture Shaped the Human Genome."
6. Wilson, *Social Conquest of Earth*, 240.
7. Ibid., 242.
8. Ibid.
9. Ibid., 213.
10. Ibid., 239.
11. Ibid., 236.
12. Ibid., 237.
13. Ibid.
14. Ibid., 238.
15. Ibid.
16. Ibid., 238–39.
17. Ibid., 239–40.

Furthermore

These forays—to be continued and developed further via aesopsanthropology.com, welcoming comments and critiques—aim at theorizing culture from a multispecies perspective. In contrast to the notion that it binds us to anthropocentrism, culture is something we encounter as we cross species lines, versions of which certainly precede the rise of our species and, in some cases, must be the evolutionary templates from which our own iteration of culture derives. But evolution is not the uniform determinant in this matter, because it is hardly sufficient for addressing what happens when "artificial selection" is practiced by different species, or the gaps and distinctions between "social species" and "eusocial" ones (like us and certain genera of insects)—or, for that matter, when culture so thoroughly rearranges the "natural" world, as indicated by the concept of the Anthropocene.

By its overlapping of human and nonhuman, culture is reconfiguring now for social theorists, just at a moment when so many other analytical concepts—ontology, affect, and speculative materialism—appealingly hearken. The advantage of culture lies in its applicability to nonhumans and the types of parallels and commonalities it allows us to recognize across fraught political, philosophical, and economic lines. There are many openings for thought here: (1) in following "culture"—as ethnographers have learned to follow metaphors—we can engage in a different mode of interdisciplinarity, with the life sciences especially, perhaps more than the humanities; (2) we can develop new capacities to challenge reductionist,evolutionary forms of thought, exactly by attending to culture's biology-bending capacity; (3) "culture" becomes a powerful means of analyzing multispecies dynamics today exactly because it bridges lines drawn around the human over and against nonhumans.

The basic point linking each of these is this: even after the human dissolves, conceptually or as a species (e.g., posthumanism),[1] culture will remain. Certainly as indelibly etched across the planet—whether as a series of future ruins (picture the forgotten cities now lying under jungles, deserts, or grasslands) or in the chemical vestiges that have changed the oceans and saturate soils across the globe. But culture and sociality will persist *after the human* because they are constitutive features of other species, as well.

But what then, simply, is culture? An oft repeated lament about the word is that it lacks a clear definition. More accurately, though, the problem may be an excess of definitions, many of which partially overlap but none of which is sufficiently all-encompassing. Maybe this is not a problem with the concept but rather with its delimited articulations, because of the assumption that it is unique to humans. That said, a countercase can be made that we are actually getting much clearer about this elusive, intriguing dynamic. This clarity will be achieved as we consider its conceptual coherence and value as its shifts in and out of focus in trying to align its usage on nonhumans, humans, and both together.

In relation to nonhumans, it's fairly clear what researchers are looking for or considering. In "Understanding Culture across Species," Byrne and Barnard summarized this as they delineated "culture as three pairs of issues," resulting in "two distinct opportunities" for settling debates about the extent to which nonhumans can be subjects of cultural analysis.[2]

> Cultural "*patterns*" can emerge as a near-automatic product of social learning, whereas transmission of richer information reveals a distinctive "*sign of mind*" in certain species. Culture can overcome cognitive limitation, and the bonus may be valuable enough to encourage limitation to close kin. When transmission is rapid, cultural traits might temporarily exhibit *inefficiency* [i.e., not "rational" nor a clear "selective advantage"], which will gradually become optimal as a result of individual learning and natural selection. The *physical products* of culture [i.e., material culture] are a sign of niche construction [i.e., place], a reservoir of knowledge with potential to aid the ratchet of cumulative change [i.e., collective memory]; and investments of *meaning* in physical objects transforms [*sic*] them into tokens of societal obligation, changing the culture itself and thus the environment of cultural learning.[3]

This rendition may seem stark compared to ethnographic accounts featuring "thick description"; there is a disciplinary rift revealed here between the sciences that favor "complexity" (such as social analysis) and those that stress "simplifying" (as in biology). But in this delineation and the ends to which this view of culture is turned, points of overlap emerge with the concept's deployment by cultural anthropologists, especially in terms of attention to the transmissibility of experience and information and the question of the extent and depth of local variation of social practices by locality.

Consider, in juxtaposition, Michael Fischer's definition of culture, admirable for its synthetic capaciousness, taking in "anthropology" over its 150-year history as a series of intellectual–historical accretions, operationalized as one (fairly) concise delineation:

"Culture is (1) that relational (ca. 1848), (2) complex whole . . . (1870s), (3) whose parts cannot be changed without affecting other parts (ca. 1914), (4) mediated through powerful and power-laden symbolic forms (1930s), (5) whose multiplicities and performatively negotiated character (1960s), (6) is transformed by alternative positions, organizational forms, and leveraging of symbolic systems (1980s), (7) as well as by emergent new technosciences, media, and biotechnology (ca. 2005)."[4]

Such a definition will be familiar and amenable to most social theorists, so it's important not to rush too quickly to affirm it as the true meaning of culture. Note a couple of things first. Most importantly, despite its prescient attunement to the "life sciences," broadly, there is no indication, either in this definition or in its article-length elaboration, that culture might also apply to, let alone include, nonhumans, as in Byrne and colleagues' definition. Indeed, it's striking in Fischer's article how frequently "anthropology" is equated singularly with the work of cultural anthropologists, seemingly forgetting that physical anthropologists (particularly those studying primates) are expanding conceptualizations of culture by looking for it among nonhumans. But most crucially, what Fischer's definition of culture forgets or fails to rehearse is that the term's application to people was secondary and metaphorical.

As Raymond Williams explained, in defining "one of the two or three most complicated words in the English language," "*culture* in all its early uses was a noun of process: the tending of something, basically crops or animals." During the sixteenth century—the word's "next stage of meaning, by metaphor"—"the tending of natural growth was extended to a process of human development, and this, alongside the original meaning of husbandry, was the main sense until the 18th and 19th centuries."[5] The *Oxford English Dictionary* maps this progression, from Latin *cultura* ("'a cultivating, agriculture,' figuratively 'care, culture, an honoring'"), as the word extended its meanings, first from "the action or practice of cultivating the soil" (1450) to "the cultivating or rearing of a plant or crop" (1580) to "the rearing or raising of certain animals, such as fish, oysters, bees, etc., or the production of natural animal products such as silk" (1780). But more than just reviewing the nonhuman "prehistory" of the culture concept, the *OED* adds to Williams's account the reminder that, by the 1880s, the term also traveled to biology, as in "the artificial propagation and growing of microorganisms, or of plant and animal cells, tissues, etc., in liquid or solid nutrient media in vitro," returning to the sense of a growing medium related to its initial application to soil.[6]

Humans articulated culture to talk about the variously yielding or recalcitrant earth—that which preceded us. And this is perhaps its core continuity of reference: the "always already," prior to the "individual," the "community," and such—in this case, always already before the humanities' demarcation of the human from everything else via the very term that previously mitigated against such a sequestered state, forgetting that culture applied to practices and intuitions that entangled humans and nonhumans. In this version of culture, cultivation is what melds the two definitions purveyed here, one directed toward nonhumans and the other toward people. Quite usefully, too, this formulation counters the "basic conceptual scaffolding" of anthropocentric thought about the environment and climate change—a mode of thinking that continues to construe the world or "nature" via a delineation of "the anthropogenic and its classical opposites—climate, soils, vegetation." As much as being a retrograde rendering, this version of culture heralds a postdualist articulation of culture.[7]

These two broad definitions of culture—one deployed to find it among nonhumans and the other equating strictly with humans—overlap to a large degree. Yes, they can be variously contrasted, particularly for the distinct temporal orientations of the two—evolution in one, history in the other. But in trying to align these two more closely, the middle zone of cultivation and domestication opens up, where culture is the product and possibility of species entanglements. Importantly, cultivation focuses attention on a gray area between biology and social analysis—where the evolutionary is not absolutely determinate, nor is the notion of a uniquely human possession of culture sustainable, because other species cultivate, too. Domestication is not an "event" that occurred once ten thousand years ago; these are ongoing processes that involve subjects like "race" in universities and corporations as well as the cultured life-forms that make lab research possible.[8]

In considering the applicability of "culture" to nonhuman as well as human, and remembering its initial derivation from practices that joined these two domains, a postdualist version comes into view, of culture no longer articulated over and against nature. This perspective has been percolating for some time in the realization and promotion of biocultural approaches, from Alan Goodman and Thomas Leatherman's "biocultural synthesis" to Paul Rabinow's "biosociality."[9] But these *fusions of biology and society* seem often to leave unassailed the *opposition of nature and culture*; the problem with the latter is that it too often *conceives of culture as liberated from a state of nature*. First, the conventional, learned character of the cultural phenomenon made possible thinking of it as entirely freed from "natural" determinisms; second, this formulation depends on construing humans as unique from all other species through the possession of culture. Cultural analysis, from this foundation, served as much as a means of critique—especially with race and gender—as of knowledge production. But the dualist articulation of the culture concept is an impediment for thinking about and theorizing sociality across species boundaries.

Instead, we need to see culture in evolutionary terms, as an emergent phenomenon that then generates the capacity to mold evolution, as in "artificial selection." This is squeamish territory, certainly—evolutionary discourses played significant roles in "naturalizing" racial and gender hierarchies and stereotypes. But keeping "nature" as a foil for "culture"—as in assertions of social construction—does little either to engage the power of evolutionary perspectives or to learn from and potentially redeploy them, via a greater understanding of the immense plasticity of life-forms and the power of sociality to shape them. The risk of "naturalizing" race and gender in all this endures, but it's also counterbalanced by the potential to eliminate "nature" altogether in discussions of culture, as entirely beside the point. We need to talk about biocultural dynamics; "nature versus culture" will continually rehearse race and gender. All of this entails a different kind of self-reflexivity—one that, without forgetting to register the influence of human social diacritics in our accounts of the world, is concerned broadly with accounting for the inescapable risk of anthropomorphizing. Cultural analysis is never freed from these, but neither is it inevitably determined by their influence and constraints.

Notes

1. For a fascinating image of what would remain behind of the human if the massive bulk of our nonhuman messmates were suddenly dissolved, see the first chapter

("The Human Is More Than Human: Interspecies Communities and the New Facts of Life") of Dorion Sagan's *Cosmic Apprentice* (Minneapolis: University of Minnesota Press, 2014).

2. Richard W. Byrne and Philip J. Barnard, "Understanding Culture across Species," *Trends in Cognitive Sciences* 8, no. 8 (2004): 341–46.

3. Ibid., 344–45, emphasis original.

4. Michael M. J. Fischer, "Culture and Cultural Analysis as Experimental Systems," *Cultural Anthropology* 22, no. 1 (2012): 1.

5. Raymond Williams, *Keywords* (London: Fontana, 1976), 77.

6. Nathan F. Sayre, "The Politics of the Anthropogenic," *Annual Review of Anthropology* 41, no. 1 (2012): 60.

7. I'm not convinced that fusions like "natureculture" will be sufficient for freeing up the cross-species analytical breadth of "culture." See Latimer and Miele, "Naturecultures?," 5–31.

8. See Aditya Bharadwaj, "Enculturating Cells: The Anthropology, Substance, and Science of Stem Cells," *Annual Review of Anthropology* 41, no. 1 (2012): 303–17; also see Rebecca Cassidy, "Lives with Others: Climate Change and Human–Animal Relations," *Annual Review of Anthropology* 41, no. 1 (2012): 21–36.

9. See Alan Goodman and Thomas Leland Leatherman, *Building a New Biocultural Synthesis: Political-Economic Perspectives on Human Biology* (Ann Arbor: University of Michigan Press, 1998); also see Agustin Fuentes and Thomas McDade, "Advancing Biocultural Perspectives," *Anthropology News* 48, no. 9 (2007): 19–20, and Paul Rabinow, *Essays on the Anthropology of Reason* (Princeton, N.J.: Princeton University Press, 1996).

Acknowledgments

This book is a product of many interesting conversations with my bio-logical anthropology colleagues at the University of Texas at Austin. I'm continually learning and benefiting from conversations with Deborah Bolnick, Becca Lewis, Chris Kirk, Liza Shapiro, Tony Di Fiore, and Denne Reed and from ongoing dialogues with my colleagues Katie Stewart, Craig Campbell, Sam Wilson, Ward Keeler, Arlene Rosen, and, most recently, Kim TallBear. The "multispecies" thread has brought me into dialogue with wonderful thinkers, such as Eben Kirksey, Laura Ogden, and Natasha Myer, among many others. A special thanks to Stefan Helm-reich for his excellent reviewer comments on the manuscript. Finally, many of the ideas here first began percolating from me in graduate school, in the History of Consciousness program, at the University of Cal-ifornia, Santa Cruz. I remain enduringly grateful to Donna Haraway, Jim Clifford, Susan Harding, and Hayden White.

About the Author

John Hartigan Jr. is professor of anthropology and director of the Américo Paredes Center for Cultural Studies at the University of Texas at Austin. He is author of several books, including *Racial Situations: Class Predicaments of Whiteness in Detroit*; *Odd Tribes: White Trash, Whiteness, and the Uses of Cultural Analysis*; *What Can You Say? America's National Conversation on Race*; and *Race in the 21st Century: Ethnographic Approaches*, and editor of *Anthropology of Race: Genes, Biology, and Culture.*